4/17/99

Steve
I hope you were
try daycare lets alot
of fun + B —
Good Luck
Alice
Parrillo

HOW TO BECOME A HOME CARE PROVIDER AND BE SUCCESSFUL

Alice O. Carrillo

A Hearthstone Book

Carlton Press Corp.   **New York, N.Y.**

Copyright © 1995 by Alice O. Carrillo
ALL RIGHTS RESERVED
Manufactured in the United States of America
ISBN 0-8062-4531-X

*To my husband, Pete,
to my children,
David and Adriana,
to my daughter-in-law Nathalia,
and to my grandchildren,
Geniveve, Sierra, Priscilla, and David*

CONTENTS

PREFACE	xiii
1. SOCIAL SERVICES	1
2. ACCOUNTS	9
3. ORGANIZING YOUR FILES	11
Facility Roster	12
Identification and Emergency Form	12
Parents' Right Form	12
Personal Rights Form	13
Consent for Medical Treatment	13
Affidavit Regarding Liability Insurance	13
Food Program Enrollment Form	13
Child Sexual Abuse Pamphlet	13
Parents' Handbook	13
Child's Pre-Admission Health Evaluation Physician Report	14
Immunization Records Required	14
Parents' Report Form	14
Field Trip Form	14
Immunization Requirement Sheet	15
Parent/Day Care Contract	15
Sign-In/Sign-Out Form	17
Parents' Handbook	19
4. EMPLOYEES	25
5. FOOD PROGRAM	29
6. ADVERTISEMENTS	35
7. INSURANCE	39
Affidavit Form	40
8. ORGANIZING YOUR AREA	41
Dramatic Center	43
Science Area	44

	Need Assessment Forms	45
	Toy Lending Libraries	56
	Safety and Hygiene Habits	56
9.	HOW TO DISCIPLINE THE CHILDREN	61
	Rules of Discipline	62
10.	INFANTS ARE FRAGILE	63
	Activities for Infants	70
11.	PRE-SCHOOL CURRICULUM AND IDEAS	73
	Directions on How to Make Recipe Cards	75
	Play Dough	75
	Activities for Rainy Days	76
	Circle Time	78
	Science Projects	80
	Songs	82
	Poems	88
	MONTHLY CURRICULUMS	92
	January	92
	February	93
	March	95
	April	96
	May	97
	June	99
	July	100
	August	101
	September	102
	October	103
	November	104
	Thanksgiving	106
	December	108
	Christmas	108
12.	BURNOUT	111
13.	HOW TO DEAL WITH PARENTS	113
14.	PUTTING BINDER TOGETHER	121
15.	FAMILY DAY CARE ASSOCIATION AND REFERRAL PROGRAM AGENCIES	123
	CONCLUSION	125
	RESOURCES LISTS	127
	My Favorite Story Books for Children	127
	Books That Can Help You With Your Pre-School Program	130

Books to Share with Parents	131
My Favorite Videos	132
Poisonous Household Items Used Daily	133
Injury Prevention	134
Common Poisonous Plants	135
Common Safe Plants	136
Foods That Cause Children to Choke and Suffocate	137
Toys That Can Cause Children to Choke and Suffocate	138
Preventing the Spread of Childhood Illnesses	139
GLOSSARY	141

FORMS AND OTHER DOCUMENTS

Department of Social Services Forms
    Criminal Record Statement 3
    Child Abuse Index Check 4
    Application for Family Day Care Home License 5
    Emergency Care and Disaster Action Plan 6
    Applicant Home/Yard Sketch 7
Parent/Day Care Contract 16
Sign-in/Sign-out Form 18
Classified Advertisement: "Sign Up Now!!" 36
Form Regarding Liability Insurance 40
Need Assessment Forms 47–55
Meal Patterns for Infants 64
Growth Chart 66
Child's Daily Monitoring Sheet 69

ACKNOWLEDGMENTS

In Chapter 1 the author reprints the Social Services forms of the Department of Social Services, State of California. The author is indebted to Joanne Hendrick and her book *The Whole Child*. Her rules of discipline are quoted in Chapter 9.

PREFACE

Day care has become a critical issue in our nation. Children are being taken out of their homes and placed with people that are total strangers to them.

As a home provider, I have the opportunity to observe a variety of programs, and have become aware of many problems that exist in day care. Today, home providers should be trained in child development and day care. They do not necessarily need to earn a degree in child development, but should have some college training. I hear home providers frequently say, "I raised five children of my own, so I am qualified to take care of your children." Home providers, please realize that raising your children and taking care of other children are two different areas of day care. Raising children does not make a person an expert in day care. Training and experience in child development do.

I raised two children of my own when I decided to go back to college to earn a degree. I found that I lacked so much training in early childhood education. I found my old techniques were not proper for raising my own, so I decided to change for the better. Slowly I started to notice my children developing properly.

I decided to write this book since I felt our community lacked information on day care in the home environment. Day care in your home can be fun and, most of all, profitable, if you organize yourself and follow simple techniques that I am about to explain. Don't give up! There are ways to survive and become successful.

Some sound advice is to visit a home provider. Volunteer your help and see if you like the profession. If you do, you are on your way to a good start.

HOW TO BECOME A HOME CARE PROVIDER AND BE SUCCESSFUL

1
SOCIAL SERVICES

The first thing needed to be done is to visit the Social Services Department in your town and ask for the Family Day Care Licensing Packet. This packet contains the first steps to starting your business. Remember that every state is different, and some states require more forms than others. Forms included in the packet are as follows:

Fingerprint Cards
Criminal Record Statement
T.B. Cards
Child Abuse Index Check
Application for family Day Care Home License
Rules & Regulations for Day care
Emergency care and disaster action plan
Applicant Home / Yard Sketch
Local Fire Department Information Form

Fingerprints for you and your family are taken at your local Sheriff's Department. Upon arriving, remember to let them know you are working at a day care, so you won't be charged. I have always used this technique and never had to pay a penny. Fingerprints now-a-days cost $8–$10 a card.

Take good care of your fingerprints. Avoid smudging the cards so the process will not have to be redone.

T.B. tests can be taken by a family physician. This will cost at least $35. The local Health Clinic can do the test for $5, but remember to call first and make an appointment.

T.B. tests take three days to clear. While you are waiting for the results, go to City Hall and pick up a Family Day Care Home Permit. This is a requirement. There is no charge.

Upon completing all forms, fingerprints, T.B. test and personal information about you and your family, return the completed packet to Social Services. The Social Services Department sends the packet to Department of Justice for a formal investigation.

If you feel that you will not have any problems with your fingerprints, continue setting up your business. Approval from social services takes anywhere from six to eight weeks.

The next step is to contact the Tax Board and get an Employer's Identification Number. This number is needed in order to send quarterly taxes upon hiring people. Sooner or later at least one person will need to be hired to assist with the children. This identification number becomes very important when getting your business income taxes done.

Workmen's Compensation is another requirement you as an employer must fulfill. The telephone number is in your packet. Call them for information.

CRIMINAL RECORD STATEMENT (LIC 508)

Every person that applies for day care licenses is required to fill out this form. The form gives permission to social services to look into the licensee criminal record.

STATE OF CALIFORNIA - HEALTH AND WELFARE AGENCY   DEPARTMENT OF SOCIAL SERVICES

CRIMINAL RECORD STATEMENT

INSTRUCTIONS:

1. **PERSONS REQUIRED TO COMPLETE THIS STATEMENT:** AS A CONDITION OF LICENSURE, YOUR EMPLOYMENT OR PRESENCE IN A COMMUNITY CARE FACILITY, RESIDENTIAL CARE FACILITY FOR THE ELDERLY, OR CHILD DAY CARE FACILITY, STATE LAW REQUIRES THAT YOU BE FINGERPRINTED AND COMPLETE THIS AFFIDAVIT.

2. **APPLICANT/LICENSEE:** SEE OTHER SIDE FOR MORE DETAILED INSTRUCTIONS.

3. THIS FORM IS TO BE MAINTAINED IN THE FACILITY PERSONNEL FILE.

Have you ever been convicted of a crime?
(Exclude any minor traffic violations for which the fine was $50 or less before April 5, 1984 or $100 or less on or after April 4, 1984.)

☐ YES   ☐ NO

If Yes, attach a signed statement indicating the nature and circumstances of the crime(s).

I declare under penalty of perjury that I have read and understand the information contained in this affidavit and that my responses and accompanying attachments are true and correct.

Signature	City/County Where Signed	Date
Print Name (Clearly)		

LIC 508 (10/89)

CHILD ABUSE INDEX CHECK (LIC 198)

Every person that applies for daycare licenses is required to fill out this form. This is to check your name or names you have used in the past.

STATE OF CALIFORNIA—HEALTH AND WELFARE AGENCY

DEPARTMENT OF SOCIAL SERVICES
COMMUNITY CARE LICENSING

CHILD ABUSE INDEX CHECK

FOR STATE/COUNTY LICENSING OFFICE USE ONLY

STATE/COUNTY LICENSING OFFICE ADDRESS STAMP
OCA (FACILITY NUMBER/IDENTIFICATION NUMBER)

NOTE: APPLICANT/LICENSEE MUST NOT SEND THIS FORM DIRECTLY TO DEPARTMENT OF JUSTICE

We are required by law to check the names of all persons who apply for a license or seek employment in a child day care or residential facility caring for children against the Child Abuse Index. Persons required to submit a fingerprint card for a child care facility (day or residential) must also fill out this form. Please complete the information below. The Licensee is responsible for submitting fingerprint cards and this form to the state/county licensing office.

TYPE OR PRINT INFORMATION

NAME: LAST   FIRST   MIDDLE

List all other names you have ever used such as maiden name or aliases:
NAME   NAME
NAME   NAME

CURRENT ADDRESS   STREET   CITY   STATE   ZIP CODE

HEIGHT   WEIGHT   HAIR COLOR   EYE COLOR   DRIVERS LICENSE NUMBER

☐ MALE   ☐ FEMALE

DATE OF BIRTH   SOCIAL SECURITY NUMBER (Voluntary, for I.D. Only)
MO. DAY YEAR

☐☐ - ☐☐ - ☐☐☐☐

CHILD CARE FACILITY NAME: _____

CHILD CARE FACILITY ADDRESS: _____
STREET   CITY   STATE   ZIP CODE

**FOR LICENSING OFFICE USE ONLY
DO NOT FILL IN BELOW**

Date Sent _____   Date Re-sent _____

☐ This is a recheck. See attached Criminal Record Report

FOR DEPARTMENT OF JUSTICE USE ONLY

The result of a name search in the Child Abuse Index is as follows:

☐ The subject of the attached report **MAY** be the same as the subject of your inquiry.

☐ No record on the above listed person.

☐ Too many possible matches to identify. See attached listing.

LIC 198 (10/88)

APPLICATION FOR FAMILY DAY CARE HOME LICENSE (LIC999)

This is the application you must fill out accurately. You must write down all adults living at home. Sign it and date it.

STATE OF CALIFORNIA - HEALTH AND WELFARE AGENCY
DEPARTMENT OF SOCIAL SERVICES
COMMUNITY CARE LICENSING

APPLICATION FOR FAMILY DAY CARE HOME LICENSE

INSTRUCTIONS: THIS FORM IS INTENDED FOR USE BY APPLICANT(S) FOR A LICENSE TO OPERATE A FAMILY DAY CARE HOME. TYPE OR PRINT CLEARLY.

FOR DEPARTMENT USE ONLY

DISTRICT _____
COUNTY _____
DATE _____
REVIEWED BY _____
FACILITY NUMBER _____
ACTION TYPE _____
FACILITY TYPE _____

REPLY TO: _____

APPLICANT NAME(S)	2. IS (ARE APPLICANT(S) OVER 18 YEARS OLD? ☐ YES ☐ NO	3. TYPE OF APPLICATION ACTIONS
	4. HAVE YOU BEEN LICENSED BEFORE? IF YES, DATE LICENSED ☐ YES ☐ NO	☐ A. INITIAL APPLICATION
		☐ B. CHANGE OF CAPACITY
	5. LICENSING AGENCY	☐ C. CHANGE OF LOCATION

6. APPLICANT ADDRESS | CITY | STATE | ZIP CODE | TELEPHONE

7. DIRECTIONS TO HOME | NAME FOR FAMILY DAY CARE HOME

8. MAILING ADDRESS (IF DIFFERENT) | CITY | STATE | ZIP CODE

LIST ALL PERSONS RESIDING IN THE HOME BY FULL NAME, AGE AND RELATIONSHIP TO APPLICANT. NOTE: IF YOU HAVE A COMMUNITY CARE LICENSE FOR ANOTHER TYPE OF FACILITY, YOU NEED TO INCLUDE THE FIRST NAME AND INITIAL OF LAST NAME OF ANY CLIENT(S) RESIDING IN YOUR HOME. (CONTINUE ON REVERSE IF MORE SPACE IS NEEDED).

NAME	AGE	RELATIONSHIP TO APPLICANT

REQUESTED CAPACITY (TOTAL NUMBER) CHECK ONE
☐ SMALL FAMILY DAY CARE (MAXIMUM 6 CHILDREN)
☐ LARGE FAMILY DAY CARE HOME (12 CHILDREN MAXIMUM) (SEE H BELOW)
AGE RANGE TO BE SERVED | DAYS AND HOURS OF OPERATION

I/WE HEREBY CERTIFY THAT I/WE:

A. Have sufficient financial resources to maintain the standards of service required by statutes and regulations to operate a family day care home.

B. Have attached fingerprint cards and the child abuse index check for myself/ourselves and all other adults who reside in my/our home or are regularly in the home.

C. Have attached - Criminal Record Statement(s) for myself/ourselves and all other adults who reside in my/our home or are regularly in the home.

D. Have attached evidence of a negative tuberculosis clearance obtained within the 12 months for all adults living in the home or regularly in the home.

E. Have a fire extinguisher (rated 2A, 10B:C) and a smoke detector device in my/our home which meet standards established by the State Fire Marshal.

F. Shall comply with all laws and regulations governing Family Day Care Homes.

G. Shall obtain approval from the licensing agency prior to making any changes that affect the terms of the license.

H. Have attached proof of the experience required to qualify for a large family day care license.

I/WE DECLARE UNDER PENALTY OF PERJURY THAT THE STATEMENTS ON THIS APPLICATION AND ON THE ACCOMPANYING ATTACHMENTS ARE CORRECT TO MY/OUR KNOWLEDGE.

I/we understand that the signature(s) below authorizes the licensing agency to renew my/our license if all licensing laws and regulations are met at the time of renewal, unless I/we notify the licensing agency that I/we wish to terminate the license.

APPLICANT SIGNATURE	CITY/COUNTY WHERE SIGNED	DATE
APPLICANT SIGNATURE	CITY/COUNTY WHERE SIGNED	DATE

LIC 279 (1988) (PUBLIC)

EMERGENCY CARE AND DISASTER ACTION PLAN (LIC610A)

Here you must write down emergency names and telephone numbers (Police Dept., crisis center, Poison Center, Ambulance, your temporary relocation site, utility shut off locations, equipment, first aid kit).

STATE OF CALIFORNIA — HEALTH AND WELFARE AGENCY

DEPARTMENT OF SOCIAL SERVICES
COMMUNITY CARE LICENSING

EMERGENCY CARE AND DISASTER ACTION PLAN

FAMILY DAY CARE HOMES (FOR 12 OR LESS)
RESIDENTIAL HOMES (FOR 6 OR LESS)

INSTRUCTIONS: Post a copy in plain sight in facility, near telephone. Return the original copy to licensing office. Licensee is responsible for updating information as required.

NAME OF FACILITY	LICENSEE(S) NAME(S)

ADDRESS NUMBER	STREET	CITY	STATE	ZIP CODE	TELEPHONE NUMBER
					( )

I. AS LICENSEE OF THIS FACILITY, I ASSUME RESPONSIBILITY FOR THIS PLAN FOR PROVIDING EMERGENCY SERVICES AS INDICATED BELOW. I SHALL INSTRUCT ALL CLIENTS/CHILDREN, AGE AND ABILITIES PERMITTING, ANY STAFF AND/OR HOUSEHOLD MEMBERS IN THEIR DUTIES AND RESPONSIBILITIES UNDER THE PLAN.

SIGNATURE(S)	DATE

II. EMERGENCY NAMES AND TELEPHONE NUMBERS

FIRE	PARAMEDICS	POLICE OR SHERIFF
CIVIL DEFENSE		CRISIS CENTER
PHYSICIAN(S)		POISON CONTROL
HOSPITAL(S)		AMBULANCE
DENTIST(S)		OTHER AGENCY/PERSON	CHILD PROTECTIVE SERVICES

III. FACILITY EXIT LOCATIONS: Draw the floor plans of the home on the back of this form indicating exits by number.

1	4
2	5
3	6

IV. TEMPORARY RELOCATION SITE(S)

NAME	ADDRESS	TELEPHONE NUMBER
		( )
NAME	ADDRESS	TELEPHONE NUMBER
		( )

V. UTILITY SHUT-OFF LOCATIONS

ELECTRICITY

WATER

GAS

VI. EQUIPMENT

SMOKE DETECTOR LOCATION

FIRE EXTINGUISHER LOCATION (IF REQUIRED)

FIRE ALARM SOUNDING DEVICE (IF ANY)

TYPE	LOCATION

VII. FIRST AID KIT

LOCATION

LIC 610A (PUBLIC) (8/87)

APPLICANT HOME/YARD SKETCH (LIC999)

Here you must sketch a floor plan of your home. All rooms that are off limits to the children, all exits from the house, yard area and hazardous areas such as swimming pools, and floor furnaces.

STATE OF CALIFORNIA - HEALTH AND WELFARE AGENCY

DEPARTMENT OF SOCIAL SERVICES
COMMUNITY CARE LICENSING

APPLICANT HOME/YARD SKETCH

APPLICANT NAME

APPLICANT ADDRESS

TO THE APPLICANT: In the space below, please draw a sketch of the floor plan of your home and the outside yard. Also, plot and label the following areas on the sketch:

1. Each room of the home (living, dining, etc.).
2. Any rooms to be off limits to the children for whom you plan to provide care.
3. All exits from the home.
4. Yard area. (Indicate whether your yard is fenced in.)
5. Any hazardous areas such as (swimming pools, floor furnance, etc.).

LIC 999 (10/89)

2
ACCOUNTS

Keeping good records is the key to every successful business. Be organized and consistent with your accounts (i.e. accounts receivable and accounts payable). These two methods will help when it is time to file income taxes.

Go to an office supply store and ask for an accounts receivable and accounts payable book. These two books will help you to keep track of what is coming in and going out. You also need to buy a filing folder that has twelve pockets (commonly known as an accordion file), one for each month. Place every receipt according to that month in the file and at the end of each month transfer the totals of each receipt to the accounts payable book. Remember to keep all receipts on items purchased from food to supplies:

Equipment   *Appliances you buy*
Utilities   *Plants for the house*
House payment   *Lunches & dinners*

Lunches and dinners should be logged under traveling, picking up equipment or taking clients to lunch or dinner. Remember not to log under entertainment, since you will not be able to deduct them. Mileage is another important record to keep. Carry a mileage book in the car, and every time the car is started, write the mileage down. Upon returning write down the mileage again. Another method is to buy a small calendar (pocket book calendar) and write down your destination and total miles. As long as proof is given that you went somewhere for your program, mileage can be deducted.

3
ORGANIZING YOUR FILES

The first thing to do is visit an office supply store. It is best to purchase the following:

File folders   *Staple remover*
Labels   *Hole puncher*
Permanent pens   *Masking tape*
Felt pens   *Scotch tape*
Ink Pens   *Paper clips*
Pencils   *Glue & scissors*
Stapler & staples   *Crayons*
                          Construction paper

These supplies should help you get started—remember, save your receipts.

Each file should contain the child's name and birth date. Type or print child's name and birth date on the file folder labels, then place the label on the right side of the folder. Another great idea is to use a red color pen and draw a red circle by the names of the children that have allergies. This indicates that the child is allergic to something (certain foods and/or medications).

In the folder, place a copy of each form that social services requires for each child. Here is a list of the following forms:

Parents' rights   *Affidavits form*
Personal rights   *Identification form*
Child Abuse Index   *Consent for medical treatment*
Emergency form   *Parents' report*
Physician report   *Field trip form*
                          Food Program Enrollment form

Social Services permits a home provider to make copies of all their forms—saving time from going to social services and picking up forms every time you run out. It is best to go to a supply store where copies can be made at a minimal fee. The library or pharmacy charges anywhere from 10–25 cents a sheet whereas an office supply store only charges 4–7 cents a sheet.

Consider buying a small filing cabinet for your folders or place your files in a box, either way is fine. Keep folders where they are easy to get to in case an emergency arises or social services decides to visit.

Facility Roster

Social Services always includes a Facility Roster in your packet. This form requires the home provider to write down every child that is enrolled in your program, their address, birth date, parent's name, work address, phone number, the date they entered and terminated. Place the roster in the front of the file where it can be easily reached. The roster must be retained for five years.

Remember, even if you have your own child or grandchild in your program, complete a file on him. Social Services is very strict about this procedure. Not having the completed files they request can result in your being put on 30 days notice. Meaning, if a file is not made on that certain child, your license can be revoked.

Identification and Emergency Form

The Identification and Emergency Form (F–700) must be completed accurately by the parents. This form indicates to us the people to depend on in case of an emergency, providing the parents cannot be contacted first. The form also indicates who the Dr. is, what hospital is preferred and if there are any allergic reactions to medication.

Parents' Right Form

The Parents' Right Form (F–995), informs parents that they have the right to enter and inspect the child care facility their child is attending. It also gives the parent's the right to enter your home if they feel their child is in some kind of danger. (Form must be posted where parents can read it).

Personal Rights Form

The Personal Rights Form (F–613) informs parents that they have the right to contact the Licensing Agency on any complaints they might have against the program in which their child is enrolled. The telephone number of the agency is on the form.

Consent for Medical Treatment

Consent for Medical Treatment (F–629) form gives the provider the right to provide emergency medical care in order to preserve the life of the child that is under your care. This copy must be signed by the parents.

Affidavit Regarding Liability Insurance

The Affidavit's Regarding Liability Insurance (F–282) for Family Day Care Homes is, to me, the most important. This form explains to parents that you do not carry liability insurance. Have the parents sign and date this immediately. The second form states that it was clearly discussed that your program does not carry liability insurance and that the parents are given the right to enter the program or deny it. Have parents sign and date this.

Food Program Enrollment Form

The Food Program Enrollment Form indicates the child on the form is participating in the food program. This form must be signed by parents or reimbursement will not be issued for that particular child.

Child Sexual Abuse Pamphlet

Abuse Index Form must be completed by the parents and signed. It states the Awareness of child abuse and tells the parents how and what to look for on their child if they suspect child abuse.

Parents' Handbook

I developed a Parents' Handbook that comes in handy when enrolling a child. In the handbook, the rules and regulations of my program that parents need to follow are explained. Each area explained is very critical for a program to run smoothly. Your handbook is your bible, the key to your success. Remember communication with parents is very important—letting them know your rules and regulations will make your program run more smoothly and professionally. On the contract the parents sign be sure and indicate whether they have received the parents handbook.

Child's Pre-Admission Health Evaluation Physician Report

The Child's Pre-Admission Health Evaluation Physician Report (F85–378) indicates the child is in good health and is able to attend day care. It is the parent's responsibility to take the child to their family doctor for a thorough examination. The doctor signs the form and it is returned to us. This form also informs us if the child is allergic to certain foods.

Immunization Records Required

Parent's must present a record of their child's immunizations before he or she can attend your program. The record must include the date (at least the month and year) each vaccine dose was received. The immunization of each child must then be copied onto the blue California School Immunization Record (PM 286, available from your county health department) and kept in your files. (Immunization requirement sheet is listed on page 15.)

Parents' Report Form

The Parents' Report Form (F90–55707) helps to let a home provider know a little about the child's background: what they like to eat, at what time his regular meals and naps are, playing experience, special problems, and fears. The importance of this form is to make it easier for the child to cope with the anxiety of breaking away from parents and be able to accept day care.

Field Trip Form

The Field Trip Form gives parental permission for the child to attend field trips. This is very important for the parent and the program. Have the parent sign and return it. This form covers the home provider in case the child is involved in an injury while on an outing.

IMMUNIZATION REQUIREMENT SHEET

Age at Entry		Total Vaccine Doses Required at Entry
ounger than two months	None	
2–3 Months	Polio*	1 dose
	DTP/DT	1 dose
4–5 Months	Polio*	2 doses
	DTP/DT	2 doses
6–14 Months	Polio*	2 doses
	DTP/DT	3 doses
15–17 Months	Polio*	2 doses
	DTP/DT	3 doses
	Measles/Mumps/ Rubella	1 dose given on or after the first birthday**
18 Months– 4yrs	Polio*	3 doses
	DTP/DT	4 doses
	Measles/Mumps/ Rubella	1 dose given on or after the first birthday

Not required but strongly recommended: Hib Meningitis***
* Number of doses required is the same regardless of the type of polio vaccine received.
** MMR is recommended at age 15 months.
***Hemophilus influenza type b (Hib) meningitis is not legally required but is *strongly* recommended.

Parent/Day Care Contract

Every parent should complete a contract (See example on page 16). The contract specifies parent's names, social security number, driver's license, employment address and phone number, contract hours and weekly fee, and that the parent's handbook has been received. The contract covers the home provider if the parents decide to quit and they do not pay, it can be proven the contract was signed stating your weekly fee.

PARENT/DAY CARE CONTRACT

PARENT'S NAME(S) _____

FATHER'S HOME ADDRESS _____
    TELEPHONE _____
FATHER'S EMPLOYMENT ADDRESS _____
    TELEPHONE _____
FATHER'S DRIVER'S LICENSE NUMBER _____
FATHER'S SOCIAL SECURITY NUMBER _____

MOTHER'S HOME ADDRESS _____
    TELEPHONE _____
MOTHER'S EMPLOYMENT ADDRESS _____
    TELEPHONE _____
MOTHER'S DRIVER'S LICENSE NUMBER _____
MOTHER'S SOCIAL SECURITY NUMBER _____

CHILD'S NAME _____
    BIRTHDATE _____

INITIAL CONTRACT DATE _____
CHILD CARE SERVICES CONTRACT HOURS _____
    DAYS _____
WEEKLY FEE _____

    IF CHILD IS NOT PICKED UP ACCORDING TO CONTRACT HOURS, YOU WILL BE CHARGED _____ AN HOUR UNTIL PARENT ARRIVES FOR CHILD.
    I _____ HAVE RECEIVED THE PARENTS' HANDBOOK AND AGREE TO COMPLY WITH ITS REGULATIONS. I HAVE ALSO RECEIVED THE CHILD SEXUAL ABUSE PAMPHLET.

PARENT(S) SIGNATURE _____
HOME PROVIDER'S SIGNATURE _____

Sign-in/Sign-out Form

A form that is used daily is the sign-in/sign-out form (See example on page 18). This form gives the daily attendance; parents sign their child in upon arriving and out when picking them up. This form is also an excellent record keeper as indicated below:

1. *Who attended that day*
2. *How much money is due*
3. *Good records in case parent's have to be taken to court.*
4. *Accounting for each child attending that day, especially concerning emergencies.*

It's important and easy to develop a sign-in/sign-out sheet. On the top of the paper, type the name of your program. Make three columns. Starting on the left, type name of child and birth date; second column, parent's signature and arrival time; third column, signature of parent and time child was picked up. (See example) The next chapter covers forms that are needed upon hiring employees. Make sure all forms are kept in individual files.

SIGN-IN/SIGN-OUT FORM

NAME OF CHILD	CONTRACT HOURS	TIME IN	PARENT/GUARDIAN SIGNATURE	TIME OUT	PARENT/GUARDIAN SIGNATURE

PARENTS' HANDBOOK

ADMISSION PROCEDURES

Admission procedures shall include the following:
1. Interview with parents and child to arrive at a decision about the admission of the child. Interview shall be conducted at the day care.
2. All children accepted for admission will be required to take a physical examination administered by their family physician.
3. Parents must provide the day care with a copy of the child's immunization records. In compliance with their county's health department, all children must be up-to-date.
4. Parents must submit enrollment packet prior to commencement. Packet includes the following:

   1. *Emergency information*
   2. *Child's pre-admission health history (parent's report)*
   3. *Child's pre-admission health evaluation (to be completed by physician)*
   4. *Child's abuse index*
   5. *At the time of enrollment parents or guardians will be asked to sign an agreement setting forth the time the child is to arrive and depart daily at the day care.*
   6. *Field trip forms*
   7. *Parents' Rights form*
   8. *Personal Rights*
   9. *Medical Release*
   10. *Affidavit form*

FEE SCHEDULE AND PAYMENT FOR CHILD CARE SERVICES

1. Processing fee:

2. Weekly fee:
    Full time child care services:
    Four hour sessions:
3. All fees are to be paid one week in advance by check or cash.

HOURS OF OPERATION
8:00–12:00   First Session
12:30–4:30   Second session
    Extended day care hours will depend on parents working schedule.

RULES AND REGULATIONS
1. Daily arrival and departure.
2. A designated parent or guardian must accompany the child each morning and remain on the premises until the child has been accepted for the day.
3. The designated parent or guardian must sign the child in and out with full signatures on the daily attendance sheet. Exact time of arrival and departure must be indicated.
4. The day care will not release a child to any person not listed on the emergency list as an authorized person nor will the child be released to a minor.
5. The day care cannot release your child to an authorized person who appears to be under the influence of alcohol or drugs.

ATTENDANCE, ILLNESS, EMERGENCY, VACATIONS & HOLIDAYS
1. Children are expected to attend on a daily basis unless otherwise arranged.
2. Please report any absences. Failure to communicate your child's absence to the day care may result in discontinuation of services.
3. Absences due to illness will be charged at the normal tuition rate.
4. Children who are ill are to be kept at home in order to protect the child and the other children attending the day care. Please inform the day care immediately if you child has been exposed to or has a communicable disease.
5. The day care staff may administer medication with parent's written consent and provide your child with minor first aid.

In the event of an illness or injury, your child may be taken to an emergency center or other medical facility.
6. It is important, for the safety of your child, to inform us of any accidents or injuries which your child has suffered outside of our day care.
7. In the event that your child becomes ill at the center, he/she will be isolated from the other children until parents or other authorized person can pick him/her up.
8. Vacation taken by parents and children will be charged at the normal rate.
9. Holidays taken by the day care will be charged at the normal rate.
10. Two weeks notice must be given before terminating the program.

DAY CARE DEVELOPMENT PROGRAM IS MADE UP OF THE FOLLOWING COMPONENTS
1. Cognitive, physical, mental, social and emotional development of the child.
2. Health
3. Nutrition
4. Multi-cultural awareness and appreciation
5. Parent involvement
6. Social Services

TERMINATION OF SERVICES
It is the desire of this day care to avoid the necessity for nonvoluntary termination of child care services. However, it may become necessary to terminate services in the following instances:

1. Failure to pay weekly fee.
2. Disruptive, abrasive, unprofessional, or abusive conduct on the part of the parent or guardian.
3. The development, by the child, of learning and / or behavioral difficulties which the program in not adequately staffed to handle.

NONDISCRIMINATION
This day care operates on a nondiscriminatory basis and services are not denied to any person on the basis of religion, color, ethnic group, identification and sex.

RIGHTS OF THIS DAY CARE:
1. We reserve the right to deny any child care service to anyone.
2. Parents will be held liable for any damages his/her child incurs at the day care.

TOYS
Children are encouraged to bring their special toy to share with other children during show and tell. One toy at a time will be highly appreciated. Please keep your treasures at home, where they are safe!

BIRTHDAYS
We encourage parents to send a cake mix and cool whip (replacing sugar frosting) so that the children can participate in cooking experience and celebrate the birthday child during our snack time.

TOUCH AND GUESS BAGS
Each class will be encouraged to bring a paper sack with a toy inside so other children can have the opportunity to guess what it is. Please put the name of your child on the outside of the bag.

PETS
Pets are welcome at our day care if you promise to take them back! There will be a schedule sheet posted so you can sign-up for a time that you can bring your child's favorite pet to share with the others.

FIELD TRIPS
Occasionally, we will be taking trips and nature walks. Please sign the consent sheet that will be provided to you during your interview. We know that children learn by direct touching and seeing so we encourage field trips and nature walks as part of our program.

CLOTHING

We ask that you label all jackets and sweaters your child wears to school. If your child should lose an article, please check for it soon. Easy fitting, comfortable and washable clothes are best for day care. Also you will need to bring a complete change of clothing for your child.

NUTRITION

Snacks are provided by the day care as a source of nourishment and as a way of introducing good nutrition and simple food preparations. Full time students will be provided with a hot, nutritious lunch daily.

QUALIFIED STAFF

This day care employs qualified and experienced supervisors, teachers, and teacher assistants to implement the program goals and objectives. The developmental needs of the children are the primary concern of the staff at the day care.

DISCIPLINE RULES

(1) Warning him. (2) Removing him from the activity while keeping him with the teacher. (3) Acknowledging feelings and stating rules. (4) Waiting for him to make the decision to return to the activity. (5) Helping him return and be more successful. (Joanne Hendrick, "The Whole Child")

CONFERENCES

Conferences will be held at least once a year. During that time you will have the opportunity to see the need assessments of your child. You will also have the opportunity to discuss any problems you foresee about your child and the program.

Let it be known that Social Services reserves the right to interview your child when necessary.

4
EMPLOYEES

An employee must have an examination done by a family doctor, T.B. test, fingerprint clearance and workmen's compensation. They also need to sign the criminal record release form and the statement acknowledging requirement to report suspected child abuse.

An employee should have experience in day care and some college training or at least 6 units in child development. Select a person that cares about children and is considerate toward their needs. The following are copies that should be placed in each employee file:

Criminal Record Statement
Report Suspected Child Abuse
Fingerprints card
Child Abuse Index Check
Health Screening Report
Personnel Record

Remember that there will be a slight charge when you send in your Child Abuse Index check and Fingerprints Card to the Dept. of Justice.

CRIMINAL RECORD STATEMENT

This statement releases any crime information that you have committed in the past. Remember that working with children, your employee's record must be clean.

REPORT SUSPECTED CHILD ABUSE STATEMENT

This form states that anyone working with children is required to report child abuse if they suspect an employee of child abuse. This must be reported to a child protective agency immediately.

FINGERPRINTS CARD
An employee must be fingerprinted before being employed by any agency that involve children. Fingerprints are obtained at any Sheriff Dept.

CHILD ABUSE INDEX CHECK
This statement releases any child abuse information committed by anyone. It is very important that your employee fills out the form thoroughly.

HEALTH SCREENING REPORT
This statement releases any health information from your possible employee's physician. This statement releases him or her as being healthy enough to work with children.

PERSONNEL RECORD
This statement obtains employment information about your future employee. It is very important to check on employment history and references.

EMPLOYEE TRAINING
You, as an employer, must provide some in-house training for your employee and it should be training you feel is important in order to maintain a successful business. In-house training covers the following areas:

KITCHEN SANITATION
Washing dishes or placing them in dishwasher, cleaning cupboards, labeling all food program items, storage of foods (canned and frozen), mopping floors, cleaning stove/oven, cleaning refrigerator, and throwing away left-overs.

REST ROOMS
Wash toilet bowls and sinks with detergents, mopping floors and using gloves when cleaning.

DIAPER CHANGES
Train your helper to use gloves when changing diapers and to

wash their hands after every change, disposing of a diaper, and cleaning the changing area with detergents.

PLAYGROUND
Train your helper to be alert at all times, keeping an eye on children and toys that might cause injuries. Also discuss picking toys up that can cause children to injure themselves.

LIFTING MATERIALS/EQUIPMENT
Lifting items properly to prevent back strain.

LIFTING CHILDREN
Very important! Lift children from the waist not from the arms. Lifting incorrectly can cause injury to the child.

TEACHER LANGUAGE
Use good vocabulary when talking with children. Remember children learn from seeing and hearing others. Train not to talk negatively around the children but to always praise and have a positive attitude toward the child's accomplishments.

ACTIVITY TIME
Train your helper how to supervise the children during arts and craft time. Your helper must not make child's art, but should be there to offer assistance if the child does not understand.

5
FOOD PROGRAM

There are a variety of Food Programs that can be joined as a home provider. Check your local social services department or Family Day Care Association for information regarding the different Food Programs your county offers. It is wise to join the food program in order to get reimbursed for all the food expenses incurred throughout the month. Buying food can become expensive and can take all your profits.

Number one rule is to keep accurate records. You are given four forms by the Food Program:

> *Children's Food Program Enrollment Form*
> *Daily Attendance Meal Count*
> *Monthly Report*
> *Menu Forms*

Always mark your daily attendance meal count form. Do not skip days on attendance since you will find yourself making big mistakes at the end of the month mainly because at month end, you will be in a hurry to meet the date line. You may find yourself with less money than you should have had. Always terminate your child, if at all possible, at the end of the week. Somehow this is much easier to keep records than terminating in the middle of the week. If you terminate in the middle of the week it becomes difficult to calculate at the end of the month. The Food Program instructs to terminate the child on the last day of attendance so you may need to make some adjustments.

Always buy food in bulk, (rice, macaroni, spaghetti, etc.). In the long run you save more money, and more money means more materials and field trips for your children.

Always serve the minimum requirement. If the child wants more then give a second serving. Remember, children will keep eating if you keep serving. Cook foods children like yet are nutritional and inexpensive. Let the children be part of the menu planning, since this gives them a sense of belonging. Whether for meals or field trips, children love to be part of the organization. Plan simple meals that look interesting to the child. Examples are:

Macaroni and Cheese   *Chicken Soup*
Tacos   *Tuna Sandwich*
Bean Burritos   *Hot Dogs*
Casseroles

For snacks always serve nutritional foods. Cookies and candies should not be served. Examples of inexpensive but nutritional snacks are:

Crackers & Cheese   *Peanut Butter & Crackers*
Popcorn   *Peanut Butter & Apples*
Cottage Cheese & Pineapple   *Cheese and Apples*
Cocktail Fruit   *Bread Sticks*
Bananas   *Carrot Sticks, etc.*

Always buy fruits and vegetables that are in season. This helps keep the grocery bill down. Sometimes living in an area where a variety of vegetables and fruit are harvested can get you great deals at packing sheds and fruit stands. I live in Salinas. Salinas is well known for agriculture and is known as the Horn of Plenty. This is an area where a variety of fruits and vegetables are harvested. Some of my children's parents work in packing sheds, so I get a lot of fruits and vegetables for my program throughout the year.

The left side of the menu shows how many areas of the basic four food groups must be chosen:

Breakfast:
(Choose three areas): Fruit & Vegetable
Meat/alternate
Bread/alternate or milk area

Lunch:
 (Choose 1 from every area):
  Fruit/vegetable
  Meat/alternate
  Bread/alternate
  Milk/dairy

Afternoon Snack:
 (Choose 2 out of the 4 basics)

The menu form is easy to follow. You write in the foods you will be serving that day. Refer back to your Daily Attendance form and count the children attending that day. Be sure and count the children eating breakfast, the children eating lunch and the children having afternoon snacks. On your attendance form you have the totals of breakfast, lunch and afternoon snack separately. At the end of the month, go back and total the four weeks and transfer the totals to your monthly report. Remember, your report must be in the main office on or before the 5th of each month, or you will not be reimbursed. The food program always works one month behind. For example: you send in April but are actually getting paid for March.

Although there are a variety of food programs that can be applied for, you can only be a member of one program. The following is a list of some of the food programs, choose one and set an interview.

FOOD PROGRAMS

FOOD AND NUTRITION
SERVICES
236 Santa Cruz Ave.
Aptos, Ca 95003
408-462-3079

KTM
3060 Valencia
Suite 8
Aptos, Ca 95003
408-688-4250

PACIF ENRICHMENT
734 E. Lake
Suite 1
Watsonville, Ca. p 95076
800-833-9259

CHILDREN FOOD NETWORK
P.O. Box 164
Ben Lomond, Ca 95005
408-724-6073

Providers must join CFN to be eligible to receive items from the Food Bank. After becoming a member, you may call 408-422-1077.

The Food Bank (Children's Food Network) is another excellent program to be a part of. This program is a lifesaver. The home provider is allowed to buy food by the pound, whether it be can goods or vegetables. I only pay $53.00/month and am allowed to buy 300 pounds of food. This averages to approximately 50 cents a pound. I think it's great, don't you?

The Children's Food Network was developed to help home providers with food costs. Food is donated by local grocery stores and are items the stores are not able to sale for one reason or another.This program enables the home provider to serve well balanced meals to the children, because of low cost. The majority of the time the program has a variety of foods you can choose from. The key to utilizing the food bank correctly is learning how to shop. Remember, only buy foods that will be used that week and that your children like. Breads you can freeze so take advantage and buy plenty.

A lot of times the program has frozen foods. For example: A complete lunch tray containing, chicken, beef, pork. Use two or three of them and mix with macaroni or rice. By doing that, servings are expanded from two to twelve children. Another great idea is the packets of gravy sauce mix. Use these packets as flavoring for the macaroni and casseroles. Get a packet of gravy sauce and pour on hamburger meat and macaroni, mix it, let it simmer. Children love it. Other packets for example are instant soups: Cream of Broccoli, Tomato and Rice, Cream of Potato, Cream of Mushroom, etc.—use as gravies. Mix with chicken or hamburger meat. The tomato and rice soup is used as a tomato sauce since it is cheaper than buying actual tomato sauce. We make a lot of mexican rice, because most of my children are from Mexican descent. We try to cook Mexican food as often as we can, because we feel that the children eat better when they are familiar with the foods.

We also experience new foods once or twice a week so that the children can taste different foods and learn that different cultures eat differently. Pre-sweetened cereals are not accepted by the Food Program as a nutritional meal but could be used as extra.

For example: serve corn flakes, then sprinkle Lucky Charms on top (that takes the place of sugar). Children love it. Old Cheerios that the children have not eaten can be used for art activities. In my day care, we string them and place them outside on the bushes during winter so the birds can eat them. Doing this activity will help children develop their small motor skills and teach them to care about nature.

Make it a habit to check the expiration date on the food you buy. Use food that is older first or food that will be expiring soon. Remember, the majority of the food from the food bank is expired but still usable. Whenever there are foods that can be stored, buy as much as you can. Example of foods that can be stored are: frozen products, canned goods, juices, paper products, soaps and shampoos are also advisable. Buy whenever you have the chance.

Rotate your food by putting the old food to the front and the new to the back. Label and date food to tell how old the food is. Remember, the food program requires you to label the shelves where the food for your programs is being stored. The refrigerator has to be labeled also. I only label one shelf in the refrigerator where I place my milk and cheese products. You must keep your food program items separate from your house items. Always check the food boxes carefully to make sure they are not old. Check to see if there are webs, tiny eggs, bugs and holes on the boxes. Do not purchase these simply because you will end up throwing it away and you will lose your pounds you just paid for. Clean all food before transferring it to the kitchen. Make sure to check and clean between folds on boxes, paper and especially the loaves of breads. Many times foods bring tiny roaches and eggs from the warehouse that you are not aware of until your house becomes infested.

A good reason to tell you this is because it happened to me. When first starting with the Food Program, I brought all items into my kitchen and started to store. After a couple of months went by, I noticed tiny roaches underneath my refrigerator. I tracked them down and discovered the bread I had stored in the freezer had tiny roaches between the paper folds. Make it a habit to check carefully between the folds, roaches love to hide in the tiniest of places. It only takes one or two eggs to become contaminated, so be smart and clean your food before transferring it to your kitchen. I learned the hard way, indeed.

Vegetables need to be washed before placing them in your refrigerator. Can goods need to be cleaned with a towel containing chlorox and soap. Remember that you are shopping at a warehouse, they are large and have a variety of foods that have not been monitored, so it is probable most boxes already contain eggs and bugs from the stores. If you clean your food thoroughly you shouldn't have any problems. Over-all the program is excellent. It's up to you to make it work. Another hint: Sign up for the morning shift (shopping time slot). Experience shows, the late shift only gets the left overs. The early shoppers get new items that are put out, but by the time the last shift comes in, all the new items are taken. You are stuck with food that has been there for weeks. It is my belief that the early shift people should be rotated with the late shift people at least once a month. In this way everyone is given the opportunity to get new items equally.

As I have previously explained, the Food Bank is an excellent program. It can work for you if you take the precautions I have mentioned. Contact your local Family Daycare Association. It's usually named after the county you live in, for example: Monterey County Family Daycare Association. They can provide more information about the children's Food Network.

6
ADVERTISEMENTS

Advertising is one area you must consider in order to get started. Place an ad in the Classified Section of the local newspaper. The ad should be catching to the public eye, be interesting and have a title printed in large letters.

It is a good idea to also develop a flyer that explains your program in a professional manner. (See example on page 36.)

Hire a couple of students to distribute the flyers around the neighborhood. Pay them minimum wage and limit yourself to one hour each. Remember, advertising is a must for your business. Post flyers in laundromats, local stores, libraries, schools and colleges.

Door to door contact is another excellent way to advertise your program. Have business cards on hand so when you knock on the door you can introduce yourself with a friendly smile and hand the prospecting customer your card. This method helps to show your sincerity in starting your own business.

Remember to explain your program in a professional way. You want your prospective customer to feel that your program is the best in the neighborhood. Start by explaining a little about yourself, the training you have acquired and your experience. Let them know you are also continuing your training in the local college.

Explain the importance of quality day care and why it's important to enroll their child in a program offering pre-school and not just day care. If you don't have training in day care, (by this I mean early childhood development classes), then enroll at your local college and start taking them. This will enrich your desires to improve your program as your business grows, plus parents love the idea of their children learning, not just being baby sat.

Pre-School Sessions
4 Hours Morning
4 Hours Afternoon
Spanish Classes Available
We also offer extended Day Care.

Sign up Now!!

Daily Activities: Each child is individually assessed and a program is designed to meet his/her unique needs in the following areas: cognitive, physical, social and emotial growth.

Our Hired Staff
Qualifications Include:

Director: Bachelor of Arts in Education
Children's Center Permit
CPR Certified

Teacher: Children's Center Permit
Teacher's Assistant:
6 Units in Early Childhood Education
Concurrent enrollment E.C.E.

Meals:
Hot Nutritional lunch and snacks provided.

Location:
1234 Child Lane
Anywhere, USA

Phone 123-4567

Word of mouth is yet another good way to increase your enrollment. Tell your friends that you are planning to open a day care and ask if they know of any friends that are looking for a good home provider. Words spread like lightening, and you should be filled to capacity in no time.

Sign up with your local Referral Programs. This is another way to advertise. These agencies refer children to you at no cost. I will be explaining the referral program later in the book.

7
INSURANCE

To my knowledge there are not many forms of insurance for you to select from. Check the local car insurance agency you do business with and see if they have a policy that covers liability for home day care. Most likely they will have a policy that covers one to six children. When you're licensed for seven to twelve children, it is best to deal with a regular care provider insurance. I am familiar with BMF Marketing in Sherman Oaks, California. This is a national agency which provides different policies that will serve your needs.

This includes a $25,000.00 limited defense coverage for child abuse plus $20,000.00 accident medical expense coverage. If you are interested, write to them and ask for information.

BMF Marketing of California
15250 Ventura Blvd.
Sherman Oaks, CA 91403-3288

Another liability Insurance is:

Forest T. Jones & Co.
3130 Broadway
P.O. Box 418131
Kansas City, Missouri 64141-9131
1-800-821-7303

Both insurances are excellent.

AFFIDAVIT FORM

The affidavit form on liability insurance that Social Services discloses is another method if you don't want to pay high premiums. This form informs parents that you do not carry liability insurance in case the child has an injury. The parent signs and dates it. Remember, signing the form does not stop the parents rights. It simply informs the parents that you do not carry insurance.

The other form I explained earlier lets parents know you do not carry insurance and in case of an emergency, their insurance has to be used. On the opposite side of the form, the parent accepts or denies the offer. If the parent does not want to use his insurance then you have the right to deny your services. The form clearly states what you expect. Remember to have both forms signed. Staple both forms together and put them in the child's file.

FORM REGARDING LIABILITY INSURANCE

We, at _____ have discussed with the parents of
_____ that we do not carry liability insurance,
giving them the choice to join the program or deny it under these circumstances.

I accept _____
I deny _____

_____
(Parent's Signature)

_____
(Provider's Signature)

_____
Date

Parent's Medical Insurance will be used in case of emergency.

I used this method for many years and it worked well for me. I found as long as you have open communication and a good relationship with the parents, you shouldn't have any problems. Remember, parents are very understanding, if you are. Being a home provider gives the opportunity to become involved, you become one big family.

Staying alert and always looking around for broken toys in the way of a child's walking path should help to prevent many injuries that could occur. In the five years of my business, I have only had one accident because the child was not looking where she was going. The parent was more than happy to use her insurance.

My next chapter will be on organizing your center, which you should find very helpful for your pre-school program.

8
ORGANIZING YOUR AREA

Select an area in your home that is secluded from your personal belongings. If you have an attached garage, this is a perfect place to organize an activity room area. If you decide to use a bedroom or a den as an activity room, make sure to remove all priceless treasures before they get broken. Remember, children love to explore.

PICTURES OF DIFFERENT AREAS YOU CAN ORGANIZE AS AN ACTIVITY ROOM

Garage Setting   *Bedroom Setting*
Living Setting   *Using the entire house*
Den Setting

Buy protection gates and place them where you feel they are needed. Fisher Brands are sturdier and last longer than any other brand. Place one between the living room and kitchen, keeping the children from entering the kitchen when you are cooking. Place another gate between the kitchen and garage door. This helps you to keep children in the activity areas when doing an art activity.

Buying equipment and toys for children is always fun. Buy equipment and toys appropriate to the children's age levels.

Pre-school toys should be big and sturdy, so children can hold, touch, and throw. Buying small toys with many pieces is dangerous because children tend to put them in their mouths, plus they become a nuisance when you have to pick them up in order to avoid injury.

Place toys that you want the children to play with at eye level. The toys should be low enough that children can reach out and get them. The rest of the toys you do not want children to play with must be stored somewhere away from them.

A great idea is to rotate your toys periodically, so the children will feel that they are getting new toys. This method keeps children amused and feeling satisfied. I do this often and find that it really helps. Children become bored with the same toys, thus start getting into trouble.

Personally I like to purchase Little Tykes which is a brand of toys and equipment suitable for pre-schoolers. The colors that they come in are very attractive to children. You can purchase Little Tykes at Toys R Us, JC Penney, Sears and Toys Galore.

Each child needs a cubby of their own. A private little area they can put their belongings and art that is done throughout the day. Label each cubby or crate with the child's name. The child's name must be written either with all capital letters or the first letter capital and the rest lower case. I use wide masking tape and a permanent pen with a thick point. This procedure helps children develop pre-reading skills by learning to recognize their name, and at the same time recognize other children's names.

Have some coat hooks installed in your activity area. The hooks should be screwed to the wall low enough so the children can hang their own jackets as they arrive. This procedure helps the children to learn direction and responsibility.

Activity tables should be placed in areas to cut down the running paths. These are areas where children can easily run and bump into each other. If your activity area is small, place your table in the center, if the area is big, place your tables at an angle. This eliminates injuries.

Always observe your activity areas to see if anything is broken or needs repairs. This helps prevent future injuries. Check your toys and equipment periodically. If broken and beyond repair, throw it away before the child gets hurt. Remember that safety is your main concern!

Label the shelves where special toys can be placed back by the children. When labeling, draw big pictures of the toys being sure to name them, using big letters. This helps the children develop pre-reading skills.

Place arts and crafts materials where children can reach easily. Remember to have a variety of materials out: glue, scissors, crayons, coloring pens, construction paper, drawing paper, glitter, macaroni, etc. Children must be given the opportunity to be creative, and by placing the materials where children can reach them, they can decide what they want to use.

Again draw pictures of the materials you want placed on the shelves.

Have an area where children's art can be posted. Children love to see their own accomplishments and are eager to show their parents. I went to the education department and purchased a certain amount of wide colorful butcher and border paper. It comes on large rolls. I created a large area on the wall low enough for children to look at and touch their art. This helps the children to develop self-esteem, which is one of the most important developments of a child, so he/she can grow normally and will be able to handle everyday challenges that will incur throughout their lives.

DRAMATIC CENTER

Learning centers are a must in a pre-school setting. There are a variety of learning centers that can be easily put together. Remember your center doesn't have to be big and equipped with expensive materials, just be creative. A dramatic play area is very important and develops social skills. In the area you should consider having dolls, small blankets, dishes, a small table and chairs, dress-up clothing, hats, jewelry, shoes, telephone, stove, refrigerator, and a small mat or cot where the children can put their dolls down for nap. Most of the equipment can be bought at garage sales and flea markets. I buy real appliances because children love the real things, plus they are sturdier and last longer than the play ones. In my dramatic area, I have a real telephone, mixer, blender, pitcher, pots and pans, typewriter, small television and clothing I buy at goodwill. Remember to cut all the cords off the appliances before placing them in the dramatic area, since children are curious and will try to plug them into a socket.

At Goodwill, many excellent play clothes can be found for the children; from wedding dresses to prom dresses, policeman uniforms, barber and beautician uniforms, dentist uniforms and a variety of hats. I also buy albums and toys at a very low cost. I cut and sew the clothes to fit the children. The children enjoy this tremendously and love dressing up and pretending.

Choose a small area, divide the learning centers with paneling, and put tables on each side to hold it up. Make the dramatic area look like home. The children feel more relaxed, and therefore, are more creative.

Save all your cereal boxes, milk containers, vegetable cans, cracker boxes, cooking oil containers, shampoo bottles, and soap boxes, so you can make a kit the children can have fun with. The children love to play grocery store during dramatic plays. They also love to play with real things. This idea is inexpensive since it is made from leftover containers from products that you have used.

There is a variety of kits that can be made that won't cost over $5. Remember to bring the kits out only when you want the children to play with them. Collect them and put them away when you feel the children are finished playing. Never bring out more than two kits at one time, since it will cause confusion and children will start throwing things around.

Some kits you can simply put together are: hats, uniforms, gloves, jewelry, belts, teddy bears, dresses, shoes, dolls, dishes and cups, and purses. Remember not to take out more than two kits at once. Use boxes to store the kits, one kit per box. Shoe boxes are excellent for kits. The following pictures show a variety of kits and how you can sort them. Label each box with big letters so that you can easily read it.

Store your kits in a closet or somewhere high so the children cannot get them.

SCIENCE AREA

The next center I will talk about is the science area. Again, use paneling to divide the center from others. The Science Center is a lot of fun, because it is a time when children can explore and experience different things. A Science center must have exciting materials and activities the children can do by themselves. You must have simple experiments the children can follow and master. Magnets are fun to have, children will entertain themselves for hours. Buy large magnets, large enough for the children to hold comfortably. Again make up some kits that will be simple and fun for the children. Some ideas are shells, rocks, plastic animals, pine cones, screw and bolts, wood, plastic vegetables and fruits, magnets, tools, measuring cups, rulers, etc.

Another excellent idea for the science center is having different sizes of macaroni, beans, and rice in large containers and have the children measure and pour. Children enjoy this activity. Do this activity on linoleum or concrete since it is much easier to clean.

One science activity that I enjoy is giving each child a screwdriver so they can unscrew different appliances and see what they are made of inside. This activity must be well supervised because of the danger screwdrivers can cause. Children will stay entertained for hours. I buy these appliances at garage sales for maybe $1.00 since they are not in working conditions. I bring them to the center and the first thing I do is cut the cords off. I place them either in the science center or dramatic play area. Remember your science area does not have to contain expensive materials. You can put together most kits without spending a large amount of money.

Post your daily schedule on the wall where parents can read it. The schedule tells parents what the children do throughout the day. They feel less guilty when leaving their children, knowing that their child is being taught, fed, and well taken care of.

Keep a record of the child's growth development. An excellent idea is to observe the children at play. Write down on a piece of paper what you observed and what the child mastered (i.e., if she/he learned how to ride a tricycle that day you write down, "Gen learned to peddle the tricycle on 1/2/90," or, Priscilla learned to hop on one foot on 2/4/89"). Place the paper in the child's folder, so at conference time you have this information to share with the parents.

The following are Need Assessment Forms that you might find helpful in keeping records of the children's growth. I enjoy using the Need Assessment Forms because it gives me feedback on the development of the child. It also helps to show the parents their child is developing and learning properly.

NEED ASSESSMENT FORMS

Assessment Forms must be updated once a month. They're easy to keep up, if you keep current information. Need Assessment

Forms should be kept in the children's file at all times. Remember, these forms are not standardized tests, they are more like observation techniques.

I believe a child needs to be assessed up to four years old. After four years old the child is pretty well developed and you are aware of the child's needs, since most of them have been under your care since infancy.

Remember this is not a standarized test—this is more of an observation technique. Some children will achieve earlier or later than the dates I have written down.

NEED ASSESSMENT FORMS

Infant: Level 0–2 years

Name_____

Lifts chin		
Generally mastered at one month	Age_____	Date_____
Holds head up		
Generally mastered at two months	Age_____	Date_____
Rolls from side to back		
Generally mastered at three months	Age_____	Date_____
Lifts head and chest up		
Generally mastered at four months	Age_____	Date_____
Rolls from stomach to stomach		
Generally mastered at six months	Age_____	Date_____
Plays with toes		
Generally mastered at six months	Age_____	Date_____
Sits up		
Generally mastered at seven months	Age_____	Date_____
Crawls forward and backward		
Generally mastered at nine months	Age_____	Date_____
Stands up alone		
Generally mastered at twelve months	Age_____	Date_____
Walks		
Generally mastered at twelve months	Age_____	Date_____
Two- and three-word sentences		
Generally mastered at twenty months	Age_____	Date_____
Identified pictures by pointing and naming them		
Generally mastered at twenty months	Age_____	Date_____
Matches identical objects		
Generally mastered at twenty-four months	Age_____	Date_____

COMMENTS:

Physical Development: Level 24–36 months

Name_____

Walks on line		
Generally mastered at twenty-four months	Age_____	Date_____
Can kick a ball		
Generally mastered at twenty-four months	Age_____	Date_____
Jumps up with both feet		
Generally mastered at thirty months	Age_____	Date_____
Climbs on equipment		
Generally mastered at thirty-six months	Age_____	Date_____
Learns to ride a tricycle		
Generally mastered at thirty-six months	Age_____	Date_____
Completes puzzles (3–4 pieces)		
Generally mastered at thirty-six months	Age_____	Date_____
Enjoys finger painting		
Generally mastered at thirty-six months	Age_____	Date_____

COMMENTS:

Language Assessment: Level 24–36 months

Name_____

Speaking two- and three-word
   sentences
Generally mastered at twenty- to
   twenty-four months　　　　　　　　Age_____　Date_____
Uses prepositions
Generally mastered at thirty months　Age_____　Date_____
Memorizes at least one nursery rhyme
Generally mastered at thirty-six
   months　　　　　　　　　　　　　Age_____　Date_____
Starts to tell stories
Generally mastered at thirty-six
   months　　　　　　　　　　　　　Age_____　Date_____
Starts to ask questions
Generally mastered at thirty-six
   months　　　　　　　　　　　　　Age_____　Date_____

COMMENTS:

Cognitive Development: Level 24–36 months

Name_____

Answers by pointing or naming
Generally mastered at thirty months   Age_____   Date_____
Matches colors
Generally mastered at thirty months   Age_____   Date_____
Matches shapes
Generally mastered at thirty months   Age_____   Date_____
Begins to group objects
Generally mastered at thirty-six
   months   Age_____   Date_____
Able to identify objects in pictures
Generally mastered at thirty months   Age_____   Date_____

COMMENTS:

Social/Emotional Assessment: Level 24–36 months

Name_____

Calls women and men "mommy and
daddy" and children "babies"
Generally mastered at twenty-four
   months   Age_____   Date_____
Possessive with toys
Generally mastered at thirty months   Age_____   Date_____

Interacts with others
    Rarely_____Usually_____Always_____
Smiles and shows positive emotional responses
    Rarely_____Usually_____Always_____
Explores with things
    Rarely_____Usually_____Always_____

Is creative
    Rarely_____Usually_____Always_____
Rating of self-esteem
    Low_____Adequate_____High_____

COMMENTS:

Physical Development Assessment: Level 36–48 months

Name_____

Hops on one foot
Generally mastered at forty-three
    months   Age_____ Date_____

Stands on one foot
Generally mastered at forty-eight
    months   Age_____ Date_____

Catches a ball
Generally mastered at forty-eight
    months   Age_____ Date_____

Jumps with both feet together
Generally mastered by forty-eight
    months   Age_____ Date_____

Responses positively to physical contact
    Rarely_____Usually_____Always_____

Separates easily from parents
    Rarely_____Usually_____Always_____

Positive feelings about himself
    Rarely_____Usually_____Always_____

Explores new things
    Rarely_____Usually_____Always_____

COMMENTS:

Language Assessment: Level 36–48 months

Name_____

Tells what is happening on a picture
Generally mastered at thirty to forty
   months   Age_____ Date_____
Knows basic colors
Generally mastered at thirty-six to
   forty months   Age_____ Date_____
Tells stories
Generally mastered at thirty-six to
   forty-eight months   Age_____ Date_____
Cuts paper with scissors
Generally mastered at forty-eight
   months   Age_____ Date_____
Draws circles
Generally mastered at forty-eight
   months   Age_____ Date_____

COMMENTS:

Cognitive Development: Level 36–48 months

Name_____

Describes objects
Generally mastered at thirty-six to
   forty-eight months   Age_____ Date_____

Is able to tell the difference between
   two objects
Generally mastered at thirty-six to
   forty-eight months   Age_____ Date_____

Is able to put three objects in order by
   size
Generally mastered at thirty-six to
   forty-eight months   Age_____ Date_____

Is able to put three objects in order by
   color
Generally mastered at thirty-six to
   forty-eight months   Age_____ Date_____

Relates meaning to scribbles or
   drawings when asked
Generally mastered at thirty-six to
   forty-eight months   Age_____ Date_____

COMMENTS:

Social/Emotional Assessment: Level 36–48 months

Name_____

Shares toys, takes turns
Generally mastered at thirty-six to
   forty-two months   Age_____   Date_____
Begins to use words to express feelings
Generally mastered at thirty-six to
   forty-two months   Age_____   Date_____
Has imaginary playmates
Generally mastered at forty-two to
   forty-eight months   Age_____   Date_____

Explores new things
    Rarely_____Usually_____Always_____
Responds positively to physical contact
    Rarely_____Usually_____Always_____
Positive feelings about himself
    Rarely_____Usually_____Always_____

COMMENTS:

TOY LENDING LIBRARIES

Another important consideration is to register with your local Toy Lending Library. The program was developed to help home providers with toys and equipment for their home based program. I found that this program has helped me tremendously. I like to rotate toys often, so children will not become bored with the same toys. This procedure is better and cheaper than to buy toys and have the children reject them. The children are much happier when they can experience and explore new horizons. Toy Lending Libraries sometimes charge a small fee once a year. This money helps maintain the program.

Some toy lending libraries are sponsored through referral agencies, funded by the state. These programs have better quality toys and equipment available for the public since they are given monies to keep improving each year. Toy lending libraries are located at the Education Department and are not funded by the state so the money received from registration fees, yearly fees, and fund raising helps to buy toys and equipment and pay staff. A lot of their toys and equipment are donated by people who don't need them anymore, so most of their toys and equipment are second hand items.

Later I will explain how to sign up for these excellent programs when I talk about the referral agencies and Family Day Care Association.

SAFETY AND HYGIENE HABITS

Put plug covers on every electrical outlet in your home. This is a must! This prevents children from putting any object into the outlets, which can cause major injuries. These plastic covers can be bought at any hardware store. The cost is approximately $2.00 for a packet of six.

Always have children wash their hands before eating. Explain the importance of body hygiene, why it's important to bathe every day, plus why it's important to wash our hands before eating.

As explained earlier in the food Program Section, it's very critical to serve the children well-balanced meals. This is a must, because the children spend more time with you then at home. Candy should not be served. There is no reason you can't serve well-balanced meals, since you are getting money from the state to pay for the grocery expenses.

Provide the children with napkins, spoons or forks, plate, and a glass. Children must be provided with flatware that is appropriate to their age. Teach children that it's important to eat a well balanced meal and reassure them that it helps them grow properly. This should include vegetables, fruit, milk, bread and meat. Maybe for the morning session you can introduce an activity including nutrition. Introduce a fruit or vegetable. Talk about how it grows, what it needs to grow healthy, where it's grown, what it tastes like, is it sour or sweet and what the texture is.

Sleeping mats are also advisable. Each child must have a mat, blanket and sheet. Mark the blanket and sheet with a number, write the name of the child on a paper and number it, so you can correlate the number on the blanket and sheet to the number on the paper. Instead of providing the blanket and sheet, ask the parents to provide them, perhaps the child's favorite one, so he/she will be more at ease and able to cope with separating from the parents. Wash the blankets once a week or send them home to be washed and returned Monday. This procedure eliminates communicable illnesses. Mats can be bought at Lakeshore Pre-School Supplies or Toys R Us. Check with Toys R Us since it's cheaper than Lakeshore.

When it's time for napping, I feel children fall asleep faster if I turn the radio on. Instrumental music or classical music is the key to relaxation. Turn it high enough so the children can hear the music and not other distracting noises.

Nap time is an excellent time for your assistant to help clean up or get activities ready for the following day. It's a time for you to catch up with your record keeping, children's files or just relax, read a book or watch your favorite TV shows. Any other time it seem impossible to sit and relax. Choose an area away from the children and where you can be by yourself.

Another great idea is to buy a step stool for the bathroom. It's easier for children to climb up and sit on the toilet seat or to climb up to the sink and wash their hands. This process helps the children become independent.

Outdoor equipment is part of the pre-school setting. Your equipment does not have to be expensive in order to develop an excellent activity time, it just has to be appropriate and in good condition. A sandbox, teeter-totter, playhouse, three tricycles, wagon and a gym set are sufficient.

The sandbox can be built by yourself or a family member. Make sure that it is build small enough to cover or buy a plastic sand box at Toys R Us that comes with a light weight lid that you can remove every morning. Cover the sandbox at the end of the day to avoid intruders (i.e. neighborhood cats). Toys R Us carries Little Tykes brands, which I find cheaper than at any other store.

I prefer not to have swings. Swings can cause serious injuries. Children tend to run across when someone is on them or tend to hang on them. I replaced my swings with a couple of teeter-totters.

Make sure children are always well supervised. Either you or your helper need to be outside when children are outside playing. Always stay alert as to what is taking place and be aware of toys in the way of the children. Keeping this in mind will help prevent serious injuries.

Provide children with a variety of sandbox and water activity toys. Children need to explore, be able to touch, pull apart and throw toys. Fill a couple of buckets with water. Children enjoy this activity and it seems to calm them down. A small swimming pool with an inch or two of water filled with toys is another excellent way to keep children entertained. **Never leave children unsupervised especially during water activities. Make sure the pool is never filled to the top.**

Buy an easel for painting activities outside or have one built, which will help save money. Painting is part of a good pre-school program and helps develop the muscles. It is also soothing and lets a child be creative.

Always have a pitcher of water available for the children when playing outside since they tend to drink a lot of water when they are involved in running and jumping activities. Children forget to ask for water when they are busy playing, so you need to ask them if they would like a drink.

A fire exit plan is required and must be posted. The fire exit plan consists of a sketched drawing of your home indicating exits you would take in case of a fire. Practice how to get out of your home with the children so they will know exactly what to do. Have the plan posted for everyone to see, especially social services in case they drop by unexpectedly. You must have a fire extinguisher hanging in the kitchen or in the hallway. Fire extinguishers needs to be tested once a year.

I have tried to thoroughly explain how to organize your program inside and outside. You don't have to invest a large amount of money since most of the equipment and materials can be made or bought at garage sales and secondhand stores.

9
HOW TO DISCIPLINE THE CHILDREN

Post your discipline rules where everyone can see them. This helps parents ease their worries about corporal punishment. I have always used the Discipline Rules by Joanne Hendrick, the author of *The Whole Child*. Here is an example of the rules:

1. *Warning him / her*
2. *Removing him from the activity while keeping him with the teacher*
3. *Acknowledge feelings and stating rules*
4. *Waiting for him to make the decision to return to the activity.*
5. *Helping him return and be successful*

Joanne believes children need to be taken through all five steps in order to develop self-esteem.

I find, by using these rules, the normal child does develop self-control. Always have someone to greet the children as they arrive. It gives children a sense of belonging and a good start in the morning.

I developed another policy that I follow after I have tried every method of discipline with a child and the child does not respond.

This policy is mostly for parents to follow. These are the procedures I have taken, when I see that the child needs more then just regular discipline. Refer the family to counseling. If counseling does not help the child or the parents are not willing to seek help, then terminate services before a major problem occurs.

We, as educated home providers, are trained to help the parent as much as possible. Seek counseling for the family and continue to work with the child during day care hours. After counseling expires or parents do not seem to be following through with counseling or even after counseling, if the child did not change, then terminate your services.

Most children are well disciplined when they enter your program, so there is very little to worry about, but once in a while there will be one that is having problems at home. That's the child that will need a good investment of quality time.

RULES OF DISCIPLINE
1. VERBAL GUIDANCE
Talk with the child, ask why he feels that certain way and guide him to an activity that will be suitable for him.
2. CARE BEAR TIME
The child will be able to go to a quiet corner and talk with care bear until he is ready to return to the group.
3. PARENT CONFERENCE
A conference is set up with parents to discuss child's behavior problems and what can be done to help child overcome troubles. Warning 1.
4. PARENT CONFERENCE
A conference is set up with the parents to discuss child's problems. Warning 2. Refer to counseling.
5. PARENT CONFERENCE
A conference is set with parents to discuss child's behavior. Parents will be put on final notice.
6. TERMINATION
A conference is set up with parents. Termination letter is presented and explained.

Helping a child to understand he/she is special and that you love him/her the same as you love the others, is a great start in changing a child's attitude. Hugging the child helps tremendously and letting the child get close to you anytime he/she wants, help him/her develop trust, which he might not be getting at home. Special words, hugs and kisses are the key to successful children. You'll find by using this often, you won't have many problems as far as discipline goes.

Later, I will be addressing issues on burn-out, which most of us go through while working with children. The techniques that will be explained will help to deal with problem children.

10
INFANTS ARE FRAGILE

Infants are the most precious things on earth. They need love and attention, so that they can develop the trust that will be with them throughout their lives. Social Services permits you to have up to four infants if you are licensed for twelve children. Remember that infants demand a lot of attention, so if you cannot provide them with enough attention, I advise you not to care for infants.

I decided to dedicate a chapter on infancy because of the importance and the awareness of how infants are being neglected in day care. Babies need to be picked up and cuddled throughout the day so that they will be able to develop a bond toward you. After all you will be spending more time with the child than the mother.

Buy three cribs if you are caring for three infants. This will help prevent the spread of childhood illnesses. Change the sheets twice a week and clean mattresses once a week with disinfectant.

I bought the cribs at garage sales. My husband fixed them and painted them. Place your cribs in a bedroom away from where older children are playing yet easy enough to supervise.

The following are items that you will also need for your infant program:

6 Sheets & Blankets (minimum)
2 High chairs
10 bibs
1 playpen
1 diaper pail

MEAL PATTERNS FOR INFANTS

	Ages zero to 4 months	Ages 4 to 8 months	Ages 8 months to 1 year
BREAKFAST	4-6 fl oz formula	4-8 fl oz formula or breast milk 0-3 tbsps infant cereal (optional)	6-8 fl oz formula, breast milk or whole milk 2-4 tbsps infant cereal 1-4 tbsps fruit and/or vegetable
LUNCH or SUPPER	4-6 fl oz formula	4-8 fl oz formula or breast milk 0-3 tbsps infant cereal (optional) 0-3 tbsps fruit and/or vegetable (optional)	6-8 fl oz formula, breast milk or whole milk 2-4 tbsps infant cereal and/or 1-4 tbsps lean meat, fish, poultry, egg yolk, or cooked dry beans or peas or 1/2 to 2 oz. cheese or 1-4 oz cottage cheese, cheese food or cheese spread. 1-4 tbsps fruit and/or vegetable
AM or PM SUPPLEMENT	4-6 fl oz formula	4-8 oz formula or breast milk	2-4 fl oz formula, breast milk, whole milk or fruit juice 0-1/2 slice of bread or 0 to 2 crackers (optional)

Babies need to be held when fed. Propping the baby is a bad habit to develop, because many things can happen. An infant is vulnerable to accidents. They can choke when drinking milk because some infants tend to vomit, especially newborns. A pediatric CPR (Caardio Pulmonary Resuscitation) course and a pediatric first aid course are requirements. Call your local Fire Department. They have scheduled classes throughout the year.

When you join the Ford Program of your choice, they will send you information on the requirements for feeding infants. To record infant meals use the same procedure as pre-school age children, it's just less requirements you need to record.

Try to make it a point never to put babies in cribs unless they are sleeping. That is all I use cribs for, only sleeping! I have observed day cares where babies are kept all day in cribs, and to me that is child abuse. A child needs to be where there is a stimulating environment,

The monitor sheet is self explanatory (see example on page 69), use F-Feeding, B-Bowel Movement, U-Urinate, N-Nap time. Record the time that the infant goes through these procedures. Show the parents the sheet at the end of the day and explain to them the pattern. Parents will think highly of your program because this shows you care about their baby. This can also be used by their family doctor in case of an emergency. Doctors usually like to be aware of the infant's patterns.

On the following page is a growth chart for infants. You will be able to learn the different developmental stages infants go through. This will help you to learn more about infants, plus it will help you deal with the parents about their child, if a problem occurs. Remember that this does not make you an expert in child development, it only gives you general information about the developmental stages.

Diaper changing is also an important procedure. Always use gloves and wash hands after every change. Change the infant on a diaper changer, not the crib. After you change the infant, use a spray bottle with disinfectant, soap and water and wipe down the area. This prevents the spreading of germs. Keep a diaper pail with a tight lid where diaper changing takes place. Empty the pail out twice a day, plus wash the pail out with disinfectant, soap and water.

Growth Chart

AT BIRTH, CHILDREN:	0-3 MONTH OLDS	7 MONTH TO 1 YEAR OLDS
Listen to speech Alertness to speech of persons talking to him—alertness to loud sounds—He starts to cry when he hears loud disturbing sounds	Alertness toward voices that seem familiar to him Responds with a cheerful look when someone speaks to him. Turns & look for familiar voices.	Listen when spoken to Alertness toward someone who is speaking to him knows certain demands—Recognition of certain objects Enjoy playing simple game.

Buy appropriate toys for infants. The following is a list of items and toys that you can use:

Rattles (different sizes)
Plastic balls (variety of designs)
Soft furry toys (something that can be held)
Toys with handles (infants can grab)
Fisher Price Activity Center
Plastic soda bottles (filled half way with food coloring & water)
Mirror (infant can see themselves)
Blocks made out of cloth (easy for infant to grab & squeeze)
Coffee can with small items so it makes noise when rolling it
Container full of miscellaneous items so infant can take them out and put back in again
Pots and pans
Variety of plastic glasses & cups

Remember to wash all toys at least once a week; this helps prevent the spread of germs.

CHILD'S DAILY MONITORING SHEET

F - Feeding
U - Urinate
BM - Bowel Movement
PT - Potty Training
N - Nap

CHILD	DATE															COMMENTS:
CHILD																COMMENTS:
CHILD																COMMENTS:

ACTIVITIES FOR INFANTS

1. Exercise the infant—massage the infant.
2. Talk to the infant throughout the day.
3. Carry the infant—take the infant out for fresh air.
4. Move infant around but keep him/her where they can be observed.
5. Sit with infant on carpet and roll toys to him/her.
6. Put infant on stomach so that he can develop muscles.
7. Place toys in front of infant so that he can try to reach them.
8. Put child in front of a mirror so that he can see himself.
9. Take infant outside and place him in a sandbox barefoot.
10. Chocolate pudding—place eating tray by infant, and let infant experiment with it.
11. Make fruit jello—let infant experiment with it.
12. Sing to the child—you will be surprised how they learn to memorize the sounds.
13. Let infant be barefoot and walk on different textures.
14. Read to infant—they are never too young to be read to. Mothers are reading to babies when the baby is still in the womb.
15. Play peek-a-boo with infant. Use blankets, hide behind furniture, hide behind other children.
16. Put music on and hold baby, softly dance with him/her.
17. Put instrumental music on when baby is asleep.
18. Place large ice cubes in a bowl. Let infants experiment with it.
19. Blow bubbles for the infants—let them observe them.
20. Take infant for a ride on a wagon around the neighborhood.

Always remember that infants are fragile and they can be easily hurt. Be gentle and caring about their needs and you will develop a happy human being. A person that will be successful throughout his/her life, no matter what he encounters. As a professional in day care my main concern is that the child be treated with love and dignity. The rest of the learning process will come automatically.

11
PRE-SCHOOL CURRICULUM AND IDEAS

As a home provider you are not required to have a pre-school program, but it is wise to consider having one. Parents enjoy it when their children are learning and at the same time getting love and attention in a home environment setting.

As a home provider, I follow my monthly curriculum. I do not practice lesson plans, but follow the monthly curriculum and focus on a theme for the entire month. Every month, a theme and curriculum is followed. I have supplied copies of my favorite themes. Feel free to make copies and file them so you can use them year after year. Add your own ideas, making the curriculum more interesting for the children.

Circle time is a must during pre-school hours. Children gather to sit, shaping a circle. Here children have the opportunity to share their toys, talk about events that happened at home and anything else on their minds. Sing-a-long time is perfect during circle time. Clap after every song so you maintain the children's attention. I have discovered this even keeps children as young as 1 1/2 years interested for a long period of time.

Keep art activities simple. Toddlers are just developing and are not interested in working with small pieces of paper. A great idea is to visit the education department. They sell school supplies at low prices. Buy large amounts of butcher paper. Staple the paper to a wall inside or outside on the fence. Toddlers love to paint with 1 1/2" brushes and make large strokes. I buy my brushes at Standard Brands because of the low cost. The brushes are located in the same section of the store as the paint. Buying brushes and paints at a regular paint store is cheaper than purchasing them at an educational store.

After the paint is dry, turn the paper around and color with crayons. Once both sides have been finished, have the children cut them into different shapes. Study the shapes and send them home with the children.

Keep in mind, toddlers love to work in a lot of space and with big items. Another idea is to buy medium size brushes and fill a couple of buckets with water. Have the children paint the fence or the house, remember water does not damage anything. It's a great way to pass time with the children, plus they are developing their large muscles.

Always remember that pre-school years are not a time for children to learn the concepts of numbers and alphabets. It's a time to learn math through cooking experience and alphabets through music and dancing. It's a time to learn about life in general. I believe that pre-school for toddlers in a home environment setting is the best way to maintain the child's self-esteem and self-belonging.

I explained earlier why it's better to place a child in a home environment pre-school program: the child has a smoother experience, free to choose what he wants to do. Plus, the child is receiving the motherly love that he/she needs, when the parents have gone to work. At a center, the routine is more structured and it's great for older children that are ready to go onto public schools.

Here I am talking about a home base program, where it practices pre-school, not just baby sitting. If the child is placed in a center early in life and follows the same routine day after day, when he/she is ready to attend regular school they will go through a time of burn-out and will reject school for a while.

Pre-school is a time when you need to teach children about the importance of eating properly. Try to sit down with the children during lunch time. I know the majority of time you are busy getting everything ready for lunch, it seems impossible to sit for five minutes, but you must make time. It is a time to talk about fruits and vegetables, why they are good for you, how they grow, and where they grow. It is also important to talk about the Basic Four Groups.

Also include a tooth brush program. Call your local dentist and invite him to come and do a presentation. They will be more then happy to do it. They will do a puppet show for the children, plus they will check the children's teeth and leave you tooth brushes, so that you can start your tooth brush program. Label each brush with the child's name. Get an egg carton and punch a whole, place the brush up side down protecting the brush end from getting contaminated with germs. Remember to brush teeth after lunch. Children spend ten hours a day in day care so it's very important to brush at least once during that time.

Play dough is an excellent activity to have in your learning center. I prefer plain dough because it does not stain the carpet. Children love to play with dough and its good for developing small motor skills by strengthening the small muscles. I am giving you the recipe for play dough, one is cheaper then the other. The reason one is cheaper then the other is because it takes less ingredients. They're both great. Play dough!

Place the play dough in a tight lid container. It keeps longer. I found that less expensive recipes do not stick to the carpet like the expensive one. I don't know why, maybe it is because of the fewer ingredients it takes.

Cooking experience is another activity I have found helpful. This activity helps to develop social, math and science skills. It is a time when children can interact with others and pretend to be like mommy and daddy. It is a time to learn to measure ingredients. Children enjoy this activity because they can taste while they mix.

Recipe cards are fun to use when cooking. They are easy to make and attractive to the children.

DIRECTIONS ON HOW TO MAKE RECIPE CARDS
1. YOU NEED: Cardboard paper, scissors, glue, colored pens, construction paper.
    2. Divide, with a color pen, the cardboard paper into four squares.
3. Number each square: 1,2,3,4
4. Use construction paper to cut out fruit, vegetable, etc. Glue the piece in each square.

PLAY DOUGH
1. Flour–As much as you want, usually half a bowl or 8 cups
2. Food Coloring–Add food coloring to water before pouring it into the flour ingredients.
3. Oil–1/2 cup

4. Water–Must be warm. Keep pouring water slowly until the flour and ingredients become like cookie dough.
5. Store in plastic bag or tight container.

I have a variety of recipe cards, from desserts and salads to casseroles, tacos, pizza, sandwiches. Children love to follow the directions on the cards because it makes them feel independent, developing self esteem which is important step for a healthy life. Place the recipe near where you are cooking so it will be easy to read, preferably near the table you are to be using.

Remember to keep these activities posted where you can easily get them. I suggest next to your monthly curriculum.

If you prefer to follow a pre-school program, instead of my pre-school curriculum and ideas, here are some excellent programs you can purchase:

HOME PRE-SCHOOL PROGRAM
23382 Madero Rd. Unit D
Mission Viejo, CA 92691
1-800-367-5258

KAPERS FOR KIDS
2325 Endicott Street
St. Paul, MN 55114
1-(800)-882-7332

LITTLE PEOPLE'S WORKSHOP
P.O. Box 43900
Louisville, KY 40243
1-(800)-626-1554

SMALL PEOPLE PRE-SCHOOL TIMES
Call collect, (303) 978-1467
for more information.

ACTIVITIES FOR RAINY DAYS
1. Block Building
2. Paper Tearing
3. Paper Squeezing
4. Paper Cutting
5. Walking on Masking Tape
6. Play Dough
7. Cooking Experience
8. Bean Bags
9. Legos
10. Scavenger Hunt
11. Musical Chairs, Duck-Duck Goose, Simon Says
12. Dancing (Using scarfs and yarn)

13. Exercise
14. Place butcher paper on table and let children be creative
15. Sing-a-long
16. Storytelling: Show picture and let children tell a story to the others.
17. Dressing the bears: Collect bears and baby clothes, let children dress the bears.
18. Make circles, triangle, Sq. Rectangle using masking tape on the floor. Have children walk to shapes and say them.
19. Jumping rope

CIRCLE TIME

DAYCARE RULES
Have children talk about accepted behaviors in day care. Read the discipline rules to them once a week.

DAILY PLANNING
Involve children in daily planning. Have children give ideas as to what they want to do during the day or the week.

WEEK HIGHLIGHTS
Discuss what happened throughout the week. Discuss on Friday what they did during the week.

SING-A-LONG
Ask children what they would like to sing. Let them choose their favorite song and lead the song. Invite other day cares around the neighborhood to join you in the sing-a-long. Sing songs that are familiar to all children.

STORYTELLING
Have children take turns telling a story that they like & know.

PHOTOS OF THEIR FAMILY
Have child bring a baby picture of themselves to share with others. Have child bring a family photo and share and talk about.

NEWSPAPER CLIPPING
Have child cut out a clipping from newspaper, bring it to day care and share the news.

GAMES
Play Duck, Duck Goose Hot Potatoe—pass an object in fast head's up–7 up motion.

GRAB BAG
Put objects in a bag–have children feel the objects and guess what they are.

SHARE WITH OTHERS
Ask children to bring their favorite toy in a bag. Ask children to guess what it is by putting the hand inside the bag, touch & feel the toy.

RHYTHMIC BODY MOVEMENT
Use an album that encourages body movement.

CALENDAR
Teach children about weeks, days, and numbers.

SHARING FAMILY NEWS
Have children share what happened the night before at home. What is their family planning of the summer (vacations, trips, etc.).

SCIENCE PROJECTS
SIMPLE SCIENCE ACTIVITIES

1. Make your own science kits.
   Rocks, Pine Cones, Magnets, Screws & Bolts.
2. Old appliances with cords cut.
   A couple of screwdrivers—let children unscrew them.
3. Large magnets and sand.
4. Water or pitcher plus glasses.
   Children can learn to measure and pour.
5. Colored Macaroni. Use vinegar and food coloring to color macaroni.
   Children learn to pour and measure.
6. Ice Cubes in Bowl.
   Children experience and see how they melt.
7. Wash toys outside.
   Children help on a sunny day.
8. Make Bubbles. (Use bubble bath and water).
   Let children blow bubbles.
9. Collect rocks different shapes and colors.
10. Pour salt in a box, let children feel texture and draw with fingers.
11. Put water in a bucket. Have objects that float and objects that don't float.
12. Have a box with all sizes of screws and bolts children can screw together and unscrew. Remember no small screws, must be big enough to hold.
13. Sea shells—talk about sizes, texture, where they come from, how they form.
14. Magnifying glasses. Collect leaves, rocks, sticks, pine cones—let children observe through magnifying glasses.

15. Water and brushes—have children paint rocks, observe the changes.
16. Eggs and salt—put salt into water—place eggs in water, see them float.
    Pour fresh water in one place eggs observe to see if they float.
17. Have a mystery bag—with a variety of small objects. Have children guess what they are.
18. Collect baby food jars—put some special water and goldfish and snail, and a piece of plant. Each child keeps a record of their fish.
19. Go outside and feel the sidewalk with bare feet to see if it is hot or cold.
20. Make popsicles—pour juice into ice cube containers. Talk about how its watery but when it freezes it will become popsicles.

SONGS

TWINKLE, TWINKLE, LITTLE STAR
Twinkle, twinkle, little star.
How I wonder what you are!
Up above the world so high,
Like a diamond in the sky.

HERE WE GO ROUND
Here we go round the mulberry bush,
The mulberry bush, the mulberry bush,
Here we go round the mulberry bush,
So early in the morning.

RING AROUND THE ROSIES
Ring around the rosies
A pocket full of posies
Hush! Hush! Hush!
All fall down.

LONDON BRIDGE
London Bridge is falling down,
Falling down, falling down,
London Bridge is falling down
My fair lady.
Build it up wth wood and clay,
Wood and clay, wood and clay,
Build it up with wood and clay,
My fair lady.

WHERE HAS MY LITTLE DOG GONE?
Oh, where, oh where
Has my little dog gone?
Oh, where, oh where can he be?
With his ears cut short
And his tail cut long.
Oh, where oh where can he be?

I SENT A LETTER TO MY LOVE
I sent a letter to my love
and on the way I dropped it,
a little puppy picked it up
and put it in his pocket

HICKORY DICKORY DOCK
Hickory dickory dock
The mouse ran up the clock!
The clock struck one
and down he ran,
Hickory, dickory, dock.

YANKEE DOODLE
Yankee doodle went to town
Riding on a pony,
Stuck a feather in his hat
and called it macaroni.

THE MUFFIN MAN
Oh, do you know the muffin man,
The muffin man, the muffin man,
Oh, do you know the muffin man
Who lives in Drury Lane?
Oh yes, I know the muffin man,
The muffin man, the muffin man,
Oh yes, I know the muffin man
Who lives in Drury Lane.

JACK AND JILL
Jack and Jill went up the hill
To fetch a pail of water,
Jack fell down
And broke his crown
And Jill came tumbling after.

MARY HAD A LITTLE LAMB
Mary had a little lamb,
Its fleece was white as snow,
And everywhere that Mary went
The lamb was sure to go.
It followed her to school one day,
Which was against the rule
It made the children laugh and play
To see a lamb at school.

HUSH-A-BYE BABY
Hush-a-bye, baby
On the tree top,
When the wind blows
The cradle will rock.
When the bough bends
The cradle will fall,
And down will come baby,
Cradle and all.

ONE TWO BUCKLE MY SHOE
One, two, buckle my shoe,
Three, four, shut the door,
Five, six, pick up sticks,
Seven, eight, lay them straight,
Nine, ten, big fat hen.

HOW MANY DAYS
How many days has my baby
to play?
Saturday, Sunday, Monday,
Tuesday, Wednesday,
Thursday, Friday
Saturday, Sunday, Monday.

THIS OLD MAN
This old man, he played one
He played knick knack on his thumb
Knick knack paddy whack, give your dog a bone
This old man came rolling home.
This old man, he played two
he played knick knack on his shoe
Knick knack, paddy whack, etc.
This old man, he played three
He played knick knack on his knee.
This old man, he played four,
He played knick knack on the floor.
Knick knack, etc.
this old man, he played five,
He played knick knack on the drive.
Knick, Knack, etc.

CLAP YOUR HANDS
If you're happy and you know it
Clap your hands, (clap, clap, clap)
If you're happy and you know it
clap your hands. (clap, clap, clap)
If you're happy and you know it
then your face will surely show it
If you're happy and you know it
clap your hands. (clap, clap, clap)
Repeat with stamp your feet
Repeat with turn around, etc.

WHERE IS THUMBKIN
(Use your fingers)
[Start with both hands behind back]
Where is Thumbkin? Where is thumbkin?
Here I am. Here I am.
How are your today, sir?
Very well, thank you.
Run away, Run away.
REPEAT WITH POINTER,
TALLMAN, RINGMAN AND PINKLE.

TEDDY BEAR

Teddy bear, teddy bear
touch the ground.
Teddy bear, teddy bear
turn around.
Teddy bear, teddy bear
tie your shoe.
teddy bear, teddy bear
that will do.
Teddy bear, teddy bear
go upstairs.
teddy bear, teddy bear
say your prayers.
Teddy bear, teddy bear
turn out the light.
Teddy bear, teddy bear
Say "Goodnight".

WHERE IS SUSIE

Where, oh where, is dear little Susie?
Where, oh where, is dear little Susie?
Where, oh where, is dear little susie?
Way down yonder in the paw-paw patch.
Picking up paw-paws, put'em in a basket.
Picking up paws-paws, put'em in a basket.
Picking up paw-paws, put'em in a basket.
Way down yonder in the paw-paw patch.
Well, come on children, let's go get her
well, come on children, let's go get her
Well, come on children, let's go get her
Way down yonder in the paw-paw patch.

THE INCY WINCY SPIDER

The incy wincy spider went up the water spout.
Down came the rain and washed the spider out.
Out came the sun and dried up all the rain.
And the incy wincy spider went up the spout again.

WHO TOOK THE COOKIES FROM THE COOKIE JAR?

<u>child</u> took the cookies from the cookie jar.
<u>child</u> : Who, me?
<u>all</u> : Yes, you.
<u>child</u> : Couldn't be.
<u>all</u> : then who?
<u>2nd child:</u> <u>2nd child</u> took the cookies from the cookie jar
<u>2nd child</u> : Who me?
<u>all</u> : Yes, you!
Repeat for each child as above.

TEAPOT
I'm a little teapot short and stout.
Here is my handle,
Here is my spout,
When I get all streamed up then I shout
Just tip me over and pour me out.

HUSH, LITTLE BABY
Hush little baby don't say a word
Mama's going to buy you a mocking bird.
If that mocking bird don't sing
Mama's going to buy you a diamond ring.
If that diamond ring turn brass
Mama is going to buy a looking glass.
If that looking glass gets broke.
Mama is going to buy you a billy goat.
If that billy goat won't pull
Mama's going to buy you a cart and bull.
If that cart and bull turn over
Mama's going to buy you a dog named Rover.
If that dog named Rover won't bark,
Mama's going to buy you a horse
and cart.
If that horse and cart fall down
You'll still be the prettiest girl
in town.

POEMS

GEORGIE PORGIE
Georgie Porgie,
Pudding and pie,
Kissed the girls
and made them cry.
When the boys
came out to play,
Georgie Porgie ran away.

LITTLE JUMPING JOAN
Here am I,
Little jumping Joan.
When nobody's with me
I'm always alone.

JACK BE NIMBLE
Jack, be nimble
Jack, be quick
Jack, jump over
the candle stick.

PEASE-PORRIDGE HOT
Pease-porridge hot,
Pease-porridge cold
Pease-porridge in the pot,
nine days old
Some like it hot,
some like it cold
Some like it in the pot,
nine days old.

HUMPTY DUMPTY

Humpty Dumpty sat on a wall,
Humpty Dumpty had a great fall.
All the king's horses
And all the king's men
Couldn't put Humpty together again.

HEY DIDDLE DIDDLE

Hey! diddle, diddle!
The cat and the fiddle,
The cow jumped over the moon.
The little dog laughed
To see such sport,
And the dish ran away with the spoon.

THERE WAS A CROOKED MAN

There was a crooked man
Who walked a crooked mile
He found a crooked sixpence
Against a crooked stile.
He bought a crooked cat,
Which caught a crooked mouse,
And they all lived together
In a little crooked house.

I HAD TWO BIRDIES

I had two birdies bright and gay,
They flew from me the other day,
What was the reason they did go?
I cannot tell for I do not know.

MARY MARY QUITE CONTRARY

Mary, Mary, quite contrary,
How does your garden grow?
With silver bells
And cockleshells,
And pretty maids all in a row.

PETER, PETER, PUMPKIN-EATER
Peter, Peter, pumpkin-eater
Had a wife and couldn't keep her.
He put her in a pumpkin shell
And there he kept her very well.

A DILLER, A DOLLAR
A diller, a dollar,
a ten o'clock scholar,
What makes you come so soon?
You used to come at ten o'clock,
And now you come at noon.

PAT-A-CAKE
Pat-a-cake, pat-a-cake,
Bakers man.
Bake me a cake
as fast as you can.
Pat it and prick it,
and mark it with B,
And put it in the oven For baby and me.

THERE WAS AN OLD WOMAN LIVED UNDER A HILL
There was an old woman
Lived under a hill,
And if she's not gone
She lives there still.

LITTLE BO PEEP
Little Bo Peep has lost her sheep
And can't tell where to find them,
Leave them alone,
And they'll come home,
Wagging their tails behind them.

LICKERY, DICKERY, DARE
Dickery, dickery, dare,
The pig flew up in the air.
The man in brown
soon brought him down,
Dickery, dickery, dare.

I'M GLAD THE SKY IS PAINTED BLUE
I'm glad the sky is painted blue,
And earth is painted green,
With such a lot of nice fresh air
All sandwiched in between.

TWO LITTLE BLACKBIRDS
Two little blackbirds
Sitting on a hill
One name Jack,
The other named Jill.
Fly away, Jack,
Fly away, Jill.
Come back, Jack,
Come back, Jill.

MONTHLY CURRICULUMS
JANUARY CURRICULUM

THEME: WINTER
GOALS
1. *Children will learn about different seasons*
2. *Children will learn about winter*
3. *Children will learn about snow*
4. *Children will learn about rain*

ART ACTIVITIES
1. Make a snowman out of white construction paper. Have children cut circles and glue them on black construction paper.
2. Use popcorn for snow flakes. Show what happens to corn kernels when they are put in a pan to fry. Have children taste the popcorn and express their feelings.
3. Use ice cubes, place them in a container so the children can touch and see how they melt.

ACTIVITIES
1. Warm Clothing: Talk about jackets, gloves, hats, boots, sweaters. Why we use them in the winter time and not in the summer.
2. Snow: Study snow. Show large pictures of places where it snow—cities, mountains, country.
3. Field Trip: If possible take children to the mountains where there is snow and let them explore.

FEBRUARY CURRICULUM

THEME: HEALTH
GOALS
1. *Children will learn of good health habits*
2. *Children will learn that eating the right foods make us healthy*
3. *Children will become aware that regular exercise and plenty of rest make one healthy*
4. *Children will learn that it is important to groom well*

ACTIVITIES
1. Talk about body parts. Talk about the importance of body hygiene.
2. Vegetables Salad: Have children bring vegetables from home –have them wash and cut vegetables. Discuss the importance of eating vegetables.
3. Daily Exercise: Put favorite albums on and have children exercise as a group, maybe one child leading the group with his/her favorite exercise.
4. Bath Dolls: Fill buckets of water. Add bubble bath; have children wash the dolls.
5. Carrot Cookies:
   Write your recipe with pictographs.
   Ingredients:

   1 cup grated carrot
   1 cup seedless raisins
   1 cup flour
   1/2 cup honey or brown sugar
   2 tbsp. butter or margarine or vegetable oil.

Have children grate carrots, mix with other ingredients. Bake in a 350 degree oven for 20 to 30 minutes until turn brown.

MARCH CURRICULUM

THEME: WATER
GOALS
1. *Children will learn about different types of waters*
2. *Children will learn that some fruits and vegetables contain water*
3. *Children will learn about animals that live in water*
4. *Children will learn that some things float while others don't*
5. *Children will learn how we get rain, hail, and snow*
6. *Children will learn that our bodies need water in order to live*

ART ACTIVITIES
1. Have children go through magazines and cut out fruits that contain water. Have them glue onto construction paper.
2. Get light-blue butcher paper. Post it on wall, low enough so children can paint white clouds. Get dark blue paint to make rain drops.
3. Take children outside. Let them observe clouds—the color, shapes, how they move and how rain takes place.
   Have child make clouds out of cotton balls glued to construction paper.

ACTIVITIES
1. Floating Experience: Supply children with a large container filled with water. Get objects that float or sink. Have children predict if the object will float or sink.
2. Food Experience: Supply children with fruits that contain water or liquid and dry fruits. Explain the difference.
3. Wash Day: Have children wash the chairs and tables. Supply the children with sponges, rags and scrubbers, soap and water.

APRIL CURRICULUM

THEME: GEOLOGY
GOALS
1. Children will learn that the Earth is made up of water and land
2. Children will learn that rivers, lakes, and oceans all have different types of waters
3. Children will learn how sand is formed

ACTIVITIES
1. Mud Experience: Place dirt in large containers. Add water. Have children stir and mix. Observe the change.
2. Salt Water Experience: Talk about ocean life. Have children cut out sea animals from magazines and glue onto butcher paper. Have children glue sand on the paper, giving it an ocean affect. Staple the mural on the wall.
3. Rocks:Discuss rocks: shapes, colors, texture, how they are formed. Collect rocks and paint them.
4. Drop Drill: Practice what to do during an earthquake. Explain about earthquakes.

MAY CURRICULUM

THEME: NUTRITION/BASIC FOOD GROUPS
GOALS
1. *Children will learn the Basic Four Food Groups*
2. *Children will learn that some foods come from plants and others from animals*
3. *Children will learn that eating well balanced meals keeps your body healthy*
4. *Children will learn that some foods could be eaten raw, that some have different flavors, and that some feel soft, hard, smooth or rough*
5. *Children will learn how to start a garden*

ACTIVITIES
1, Carrot Raisin Man: Introduce carrots to children. Have children feel the carrots and talk about them (are they smooth or rough? Are they short or long? Are they hairy, etc?). Have children talk about the color, taste, etc. Cut some carrots into small pieces and place on table—have children form a carrot man—supply some raisins for eyes. Have children eat their carrot man.
2. Green Fruits—Yellow Fruits: Introduce yellow and green vegetables and fruits. Talk about the fruits and vegetables (how they grow, where they grow, what color they are, and how they taste: sour, or sweet?).
3. Butter: Use whipping cream, small jars, and yellow food coloring. Pour whipping cream into jars. Put lid on tightly. Have children shake until it becomes butter. Add a couple of drops of yellow food coloring. Have children enjoy the butter with saltine crackers.

4. Field Trip: Grocery in your neighborhood. Buy fruits and vegies, bring back and wash them. Enjoy them with sour cream.
5. Garden: Grow you own small garden. Carrots and beans are easy to grow, as well as pumpkins, squash.
6. Storytelling: Tell the children about a boy who ate veg and fruits, milk, cheese, meats and breads and grew healthy, handsome and strong. Stress how he developed strong bones and teeth, shinny hair, and nice complexion.

JUNE CURRICULUM

THEME: CITY AND THE COUNTY
GOALS
1. Children will become aware that the city life is busy compared to country life
2. Children will learn that the city has more buildings
3. Children will begin to realize that the life in the city is faster paced

ART ACTIVITIES
1. Using posters, books, and magazines, talk about the city. Extend learning on the different types of buildings, high rises, stores, streets, freeways, traffic and the people.
2. City Clothes: Have a child lay down on butcher paper. Trace the body and staple the sides together and stuff with paper. Cut out a tie, jacket, pants, etc. so that children can dress the way people dress in the city.
3. Country Clothes: Have a child lay down on butcher paper. Trace the child (remember make 2). Staple together. Cut out a shirt, overalls, boots and hankerchief so the children can dress like a farmer. Discuss the difference between country clothes and city clothes.
   Display pictures of people working on the farm—talk about what they do and compare to city work.
4. Mural: Have children cut out pictures from magazines that show people working out in the country. Have them glue on construction paper.

JULY CURRICULUM

THEME: SUMMER FUN
GOALS
1. Children will learn to swim
2. Children will learn about signal lights
3. Children will learn about trains
4. Children will learn about watermelons, how they grow, what they taste like, how they feel, etc.

ACTIVITIES
1. Enroll children in a swimming program
2. Street Safety: Have children learn the signal lights. Cut out circles (green, red, yellow) and have children glue them on construction paper.
3. Field Trip: Take children to a car lot—talk about different transportations.

    Take children to a train station—have them observe the train when they come in.

    Take children to a shed where trucks are being loaded with vegetables ready to be taken to the grocery store.
4. Watermelon Eating Contest:Cut watermelon pieces and place on table. Have children sit. Time the children to see who eats the watermelon the fastest.

AUGUST CURRICULUM

THEME: TRANSPORTATION
GOALS
1. *Children will learn about different transportation methods*
2. *They will be able to learn the names of different transportations*
3. *Children will learn safety rules when crossing a street*

ART ACTIVITIES
1. Collage:Have children cut out a variety of cars and trucks from magazines. Have them glue them on construction paper. Ask children about the picture—write down what the children say.
2. Parachute: Make your own parachute out of an old king size sheet. Cut a round circle in the middle of the sheet to allow air flow. Place it with light balls, preferably balloons, nerf balls or light rubber balls.
   Have children grab the parachute along the edges. Have children lift parachute up and down to balance the balls.
3. Explore Shells and Rocks: Take children to the beach. Collect shells and rocks. Bring them back to daycare and study them. What color are they? Does it feel smooth or rough? What shape are they? Do they smell? Paint the rocks different colors.

ACTIVITIES
1. Counting Cars and Trucks: Have children go to front yard. Have them count all the cars and trucks in the neighborhood.
2. Picnic: Plan a picnic. Take a week to discuss what to take, how to act and how to follow rules when at the park. Play ball at the park.
3. Water Activity at Day care: Buy a small swimming pool—fill it with only a couple of inches of water—let children sit in it and bathe dolls.

SEPTEMBER CURRICULUM

THEME: ENVIRONMENT
GOALS
1. *Children will become aware that the environment is composed of plants, animals, water, wind, birds, reptiles, etc.*
2. *Children will understand that the weather has an impact on the environment*
3. *Children will learn of seasonal changes*

ART ACTIVITIES:
1. Animal collage
2. Plant collage
3. Make butterflies
4. Make bee hives
5. Make a bumble bee
6. Paint rocks and shells
7. Make kites
8. Make a farm and animals

ACTIVITIES
1. Talk about plants, animals, water, birds, reptiles, etc.
2. Take children to the beach, collect shells and rocks.
3. Take children to a zoo or museum.
4. Take children to library. Let the check out books about animals and plants.

Go out and catch butterflies, observe them and then let them go.

OCTOBER CURRICULUM

THEME: HALLOWEEN
GOALS
1. *The students learn of social events*
2. *Students will learn symbols of Halloween*
3. *Students will learn to follow safety rules*
4. *Students will learn that Halloween is a time to have fun*

ART ACTIVITIES

1. Pumpkin Experience: Have children sensorially learn about the pumpkin. Help them cut the pumpkin, take pulp out, feel it, talk about it, make a Jack O Lantern. For follow up activity, have children make their own pumpkin using modelling clay or play dough. Color them and record language.
2. Witches Hat: Discuss witches hat shapes. Talk about the concepts of tall, short, fat, skinny, etc. Have children make cones with black construction paper. Decorate using sticks, stars, circles, etc.
3. Paper Bag Pumpkin: Stuff paper bags with newspaper. Tie off top with rubber band. Have children paint them orange and glue on the features.
4. Ghosts: Make ghost out of white construction paper. Have children draw a happy face on the ghost.
5. Spider Web: Draw a spider web on white construction paper, pour glue along lines and have children line with black yarn on glue. Draw favorite Halloween pictures of bats, spiders, witches, cats, etc. Cut and glue them on the spider web.

NOVEMBER CURRICULUM

THEME: HARVEST
Harvest is associated with Thanksgiving. Therefore the following ideas could be blended with the theme Thanksgiving.
GOALS
1. *Children will learn the difference between fruits and vegetables.*
2. *Children will learn that some foods need to be cooked before eaten. Also, they will learn that some vegetables can be eaten raw.*
3. *Children will learn about "harvesting." What it means and time of celebration in various cultures around the world.*
4. *Children will learn about potato plants. How to plant them, how to care for them, etc.*

ACTIVITIES
1. Potato Plant: Put a little dirt in the bottom of the cup. Drop the potato chunk into the cup. Cover with more dirt. Water well. Have each child plant his own potato chunk. Afterwards, place the cups on the science center shelf to grow. Have each child clean up his own area.
2. Bean Collage: Demonstrate how to make a bean collage with the assortment of beans (including the fresh ones). Distribute the paper and glue. Then let the children make a wild and wonderful bean collage with the piles of beans.
3. Horn of Plenty: Hold up picture of Horn-of-Plenty.
   What do you suppose this is?
   This is called a horn of plenty, and it is usually a sign of a good harvest. Around this time of year, you might see a horn of plenty picture in the grocery store. This is their way of

saying they have a good harvest of fruits and vegetables. Have each child name his favorite fruit and vegetable. Quickly sketch the outline or have the child choose from a selection of pre-drawn fruits and vegetables.
4. Fruit Salad: Have children bring one fruit. You furnish the cool whip. Talk about the different fruits. Have children cut all the fruits–supervise the children very carefully during the cutting process.

THANKSGIVING

THEME:
GOALS
> 1. *Children will learn what Thanksgiving means*
> 2. *Become familiar with the first American Thanksgiving*
> 3. *Realize that Thanksgiving is commonly associated with harvest celebration and good things to eat*

ACTIVITIES
1. Paper Bag Turkeys: Have the children stuff the lunch bags with newspaper. Paint the bag brown. Let it dry. Cut out colorful feathers. Glue feathers to bag. Also cut out the head and have children glue it in the bag creating a turkey.
2. Indian Headbands: Make head bands with construction paper. Cut out colorful feathers and bands. Glue feathers to band. Wear them during your Thanksgiving dinner.
3. Turkey: Display a picture of a real turkey. Discuss the colors in the feathers and the size of bird. Also discuss the shape of the bird and how they wobble when the walk.
   Have children trace their hands on construction paper add legs, beak, eyes, etc. Have children color the feathers.
4. Pinecomb Turkey: Get small pinecombs. Cut out the heads and colorful feathers. Stick feathers into the pinecombs and glue. They make beautiful center pieces for Thanksgiving dinner.
5. Thanksgiving Dinner: Have a family style dinner. Set the tables with flatware and napkins. Place food on the center and have children serve themselves.
6. Ambrosia Salad:

Ingredients:
- 1 can mixed fruit,
- 1 container sour cream (small),
- 1 cup mini marshmallows,
- 1/2 cup coconut

Drain the fruits and mix with the rest of the ingredients.

7. Giant Turkey: Cut out a giant turkey from a large butcher paper. Using multi-color paint, let the children print their hands on the turkey. Mark the eyes and display the giant turkey.

8. (Pumpkin Pies):

Ingredients:

1 pie crust,

1/2 cup canned pumpkin pie mix
- 2 tbsp evap. milk,
- 1 small egg,
- 1 tbsp. sugar

Mix pumpkin and milk thoroughly. Add eggs, and mix again. Pour into pie crust and bake at 350° F for 45 minutes.

DECEMBER CURRICULUM

THEME: CHRISTMAS
GOALS
1. Children will learn of the social events
2. Children will learn that Christmas is a time to give gifts and greet others
3. Children will learn to understand that Christmas is a holiday season
4. Children will become aware that Christmas is celebrated around the world

ACTIVITIES
1. Christmas Tree: Have children cut two identical shapes of a Christmas tree from poster board. In one, make a slit in the middle, from top to the center, and in the other slit should be from bottom to the center of the trunk. Have children pass one over the other through the slit. Glue them together to keep in place. Have children fix it on a wooden or clay base. Have children decorate the tree with sequins, stars, glitter, etc.
2. Christmas Wreath: Using collage material: paper plates, macaroni, buttons, pine cones, old ribbons, bows, holy sprigs, olive leaves or any other material of your choice, glue or paste to a rim of a thick paper plate. When gluing, make sure the children arrange them to get the appearance of a wreath. When dry, spray silver or gold paint (optional).
3. Christmas Stockings: Place together two old Christmas cards of same size, blank sides inward. Cut the shape of a stocking and punch holes using the hole puncher. Have children pass a string or yarn lacing the stockings.
4. Bells: (From paper cups) using small cups (yogurt, ice cream, water, styrofoam) have children glue tissue papers to cover

the surface. Make a hole on the bottom, pass a string through, and hang on the tree.
5. Chains: Use different shape macaroni. Dye them with food coloring and have children string them together to make long chains. Join together and use to decorate the tree.
6. Storytelling: Go to library. Check out books on how Christmas is celebrated around the world.
7. Christmas Dinner: Set up a table. Decorated with crafts that the children made. Let children choose what they want to eat. Set up the table family style. Let children serve themselves and pass bowl around the table, giving the children the opportunity to choose what they want to eat. Encourage children to try a little bit of everything.

12
BURNOUT

I felt I needed to include this topic in my book. I know from experience that we all go through this pretty often when working with children. I will be giving you ways on how to cope with children and ways to ease your tensions. First of all, set aside some time for yourself. Try to rest at least twice a day, maybe two short breaks or one half-hour break. Remember that you as a home provider are allowed to be away from the business 20% of the time you operate. For instance, if you're open ten hours, you are allowed 2 hours for yourself. This is your time to do whatever you want, but if you're like most of us, we start to feel guilty when we are away from the children, so we end up not using the time constructively.

Burnout seems to creep up slowly; you find yourself tired, restless, irritable, frustrated, and bored. Then you realize it is burnout. If we would only take time away from the children and rest, we would not go through burnout as often as we do.

Another excellent time to take a break is during nap time. Maybe you can read a book or just meditate, closing your eyes and imagining yourself somewhere else. Meditation is a good way to relax mentally and physically.

Doing exercise with the children can release stress. Make time during the morning sessions to stretch, jump, hop, bend, crawl, roll, etc. This will help you tremendously. I know, because I have added this to my daily routine. Taking a nature walk with the children is very relaxing, or maybe even going by yourself. Give yourself a chance to get away from the children and think about things you would love to do. Ride your bike and maybe put on an infant seat and have the children take turns going with you. Children love to go for walks and bike rides. They can be out all day long if you let them.

Remember pre-school years are the time in a child's life to learn about nature and living things. It's a time to learn about animals, flowers, mountains, water, snow, sun, earth and family. It is a time to learn about life!

Pre-School years are not years that children must learn their abc's and numbers through drill exercise. They are years that children learn abc's and numbers through music and dancing. Offering the children a place where they can come to play and develop normally, mentally and physically, is the best pre-school program you can have. But in order to offer this to your children you must be able to take time out for yourself. Rest, so that you can prevent burnout!

When you feel frustrated toward the children, get up and tell your assistant you are going for a short walk and leave. When you return, you'll feel much better, plus the children will be happier to see you happy again.

Working with children can be very stressful, so you must find ways to get away for a short period of time, even if it's just to go outside to water the grass.

Form a group of ladies that can call each other for support. Sometimes we need to talk to someone about the problems that are going on in our day care and who better than women who are experienced in day care. I have some friends I call when I feel frustrated with my work and just talking it out helps you to realize that you are not the only one with problems. You find out that you are normal after all.

We as women tend to lose our self-esteem too easily. We need each other for pep talks and to encourage ourselves to continue.

Joining your local Family Day Care Association is another way to release stress. The monthly meetings are developed to help you obtain information on a variety of topics that are helpful to you as a home provider. Belonging to the Association has helped me realize we are not just babysitters; we are professionals trained to care for children. So, ladies, it's wise to join your local Association and become an active member.

One chapter is on why it's important to join an association. I talk about what it offers, but before we get into that I want to start my next chapter, on How to Deal With Parents.

13
HOW TO DEAL WITH PARENTS

Communication is the number one priority when it comes to parents. Having a good relationship with the parents helps to minimize stress. Be honest, explain what is happening, and what you are going to do to resolve the matter. You also should ask your parents if they have better suggestions and tell them you are willing to work with them, so that they, as parents, can be happy with the results. Remember to be consistent and firm, yet understanding and caring for their needs. Parents can be friendly and understanding if you are friendly and understanding!

Once in awhile you'll end up with a parent that is stubborn and does not want to understand why you are taking action against the matter. Just continue to do what needs to be done and be firm about it. Then tell the parent that he has a choice, to follow through or be suspended until it is resolved. Most parents will abide by the rules. If a certain parent is determined not to follow through I feel he/she is not worth having in the program. The best thing to do is to terminate your services. If there is a complaint from a parent about a certain child, for example:

Parent: "My daughter told us that Johnny pulled down her panties yesterday".

Teacher: I will have a talk with Johnny today about the matter. Please understand that children tend to explore with each other, but it doesn't mean he is doing it because of sexual arousal. It is just a developmental stage. I will certainly have a talk with Johnny today.

Most parents will agree with you and continue on their way. 99 percent of the time a normal child will quit doing that and will amuse himself by directing him to another activity he finds interesting. Never approach a child with a negative attitude, no matter what the situation is. If you see Johnny pulling someone's panties down, just explain to him that we don't do that at the center, and that playing with the puzzles is a lot more fun, and guide Johnny to the puzzles.

Money is another major problem in our profession. People tend to take advantage of us because they think that our profession is not as important as theirs. Let parents know that payments are just as important to us as their wages are to them. Also, make parents aware that your job is a profession, and you would prefer to be known as a Home Provider, not a baby-sitter.

A Home Provider is a person that offers excellent day care which includes pre-school programs plus an environment that is safe and an environment where children can grow and develop normally. A baby sitter is a person that is not trained or experienced in child development. That is a point that I always stress to people when telling the parents the difference between the two, and you will notice their attitudes toward day care change. Parents will become easier to handle when problems occur, no matter what the situation is.

A great idea is to post a sign that states Pay Day or Fees are due. Post it a day ahead so that parents will be prepared when the time comes. Parents tend to forget when it is time to pay their fees, I don't know why, maybe it is because they don't see us as professionals or they don't take us seriously. They put us at the end of their list when it comes to payments due.

Gossip is another major problem that can be stopped, if you continue to act professionally about it. If a parent approaches you with a rumor she heard from around the neighborhood, for example:

Parent: I heard that the babies cry a lot. My friend lives in the neighborhood and she hears the babies all the time. Is this true?
Teacher: Well, children tend to cry about one thing or another. That is part of my profession. I become alert

when one child is crying all the time, but if different children cry for one reason or another, I become passive about it. Usually, the child will quit within minutes. Sometimes children will just cry because someone took a toy or doesn't let them play.

Remember that parents have the right to drop in and visit your day care at any time, so be prepared. Never raise your voice toward the children, because you never know who is walking by, or entering the premises. Keeping your voices at a low tone is a good habit to get into. I know sometimes it is hard, but always keep in mind that parents can be standing right by your side and then you will have some explaining to do. So stay on the safe side, and keep voice at a low tone.

If you constantly raise your voice you will find that it is more difficult for you to handle the children. You will also find that you have created hyperactive children, unhappy children, and cry babies.

Yelling at the children is not very professional in the first place. If you happen to have that type of attitude toward the children, I advise you quit the profession before it is to late. Yelling sometimes can lead to other major problems.

Sometimes we tend to raise our voices for the purpose of showing authority, which is okay once in awhile, but when it becomes a habit, it becomes serious. Always keep in mind: I am not going to raise my voice today. After awhile you have developed the habit of not raising your voice.

Put together a Resource Library for your parents. They enjoy that. What I did is visited our local Health clinic and picked up a variety of information about drugs, nutrition, health, abuse, alcoholism, transmitted diseases, childhood communicable diseases.

I made a bulletin and posted one pamphlet of each topic. I went to the office of Education and bought some wide butcher paper, trimming border and stapled it around the butcher paper. I used their cutting machine to cut out Parent Resource. Remember to use bright colors to attract the eye.

Once a month I distributed one pamphlet to the parents. They enjoy reading the information and sometimes they learn about something they were not aware of. I think this extra service to your parents is a great way to keep a good relationship going between you and the parents. Plus it shows the parents that you care. You can also let them know that if they have any problems you can refer them to agencies where they can seek help or, if they prefer, more information on a certain topic.

Another excellent idea is a Parent's Bulletin Board. Make the bulletin board just like the Parent's Resource Library. On the parent's bulletin board you can post current information you want parents to be aware of. Keep a log book where you can write down what the children did throughout the day. Also on the log write down any unusual behavior or accidents the children incurred at the center. Hang the log book where the parents can easily have excess to it. This gives the parent an opportunity to see what their children did throughout the day. Always date and sign your name.

Every three months it is a good idea to have a parent meeting. Maybe have a speaker from the Health Department come and do a presentation on a topic you feel is worth presenting to the parents. During the meeting it is your chance to bring out any problems you have so the parents can give input, since it is their children you are caring for. The Health Department and other local agencies are more than happy to do presentations free of charge.

Once a year I plan a big party for my parents and children. I usually have it at the end of the summer. We have plenty of food, which I supply, and a variety of games. It is a time to have fun with the children, and socialize with the parents. Some ideas for your summer party are the following: Food: hot dogs, hamburgers, salads, chips, punch, ice cream cones. Games such as: Sack races, bingo, water balloons, musical chairs, sing-a-long. Art and crafts such as: table set up with scissors, glue, beads, macaroni, crayons, so that they can do free art. Beads and string so they can thread. Cookies that the children bakes so that they can frost and decorate them.

Keep your party simple, maybe play two games plus sing-a-long involving the parents. For food, hot dogs, chips, punch and ice cream cones will do.

Have your children make the invitations. Children have more fun planning and getting involved and besides, the parents love it when their child makes something special, no matter what it is. Distribute your invitation Monday if the party is on Friday evening, giving the parents enough time to plan. Always remind parents by posting the event, the date and the time close to where they sign their children in and out.

Picture Day is also big with parents. Call your local studio and ask if they do class pictures of pre-schoolers. Ask if the person that comes out to take the pictures has experience photographing children. If he doesn't ask for someone that has the experience and patience. The reason I'm telling you to be aware who they send is because I had a bad experience with a photographer that didn't have the patience or the personality to deal with children. The pictures were not taken professionally and parents became very upset.

Thanksgiving Luncheon is a big hit. We, the children and staff, prepare all the trimmings and decorations for the luncheon. We stuff a fryer and bake our pies, decorate the table and have our home-style meal. Everyone gets to serve themselves. We pass around the bowls and plates of foods, giving the child the choice if he wants that certain food or not. We also make pilgrim hats and Indian hats and talk about Thanksgiving and the meaning behind it.

Invite the parents to the Luncheon. They love to see their children dressed up, plus gives it them time to spend with their children during the lunch, which they can't normally do.

Invite a different parent once a month to come and eat lunch with their child. Let them know when it is lunch time and tell them to call before coming so you will be prepared. This helps release some pressure off the parents. Parents tend to feel guilty when working long hours, so this gives them the opportunity to spend time with their child during the day, when normally they wouldn't be able to. Have a space outside where Mom or Dad and Johnny can eat by themselves, so that they can interact comfortably. Parents will appreciate your concern.

A Christmas program is also a big hit with the parents. Plan your program two weeks before Christmas. An evening program is a great success because that's when both parents can attend. Again, have the children make the invitations and keep the party simple. Have the children prepare for the party one week before, baking cookies, making decorations, cleaning the center. Parents enjoy eating goodies that their children make.

Set a table where children and parents can go and decorate their own cookies. Sugar cookies are the best to bake for the big event, but remember to leave them plain so that the children and parents can decorate. Buy frosting that comes in tubes so the children can just squeeze it out and get sprinkle candy that comes in tiny plastic containers, so that the children can shake the container and sprinkle candy on top of frosting. This art activity is fun to do plus parents and children enjoy eating the cookies they have decorated.

Cookies, cupcakes, punch and coffee is plenty to serve at your Christmas party. Have Santa Claus visit for one hour, which is plenty of time. Call your local family day care association for information on renting a Santa Claus, usually they have a certain Santa that visits the day cares for a small fee. What I did last year is bought small gifts for each of my children, put them in a bag and placed them outside so that Santa could pick-up and bring them in. The children were flabbergasted.

Have the children present their Christmas program to the parents before Santa arrives. Then have a sing-a-long with parents participating. This is always fun! Christmas is one of the best times of the year. I love everything about Christmas, the glitter, the lights, the decorations, the children dressing up, the music and the friendly attitude everyone has toward each other.

Your Easter party is also a big event. Have the children make their own Easter Baskets. Buy regular size lunch bags, have the children either paint the bags or color with crayons and glue different things on them, preferably cut our bunnies, eggs, and grass, or different shapes. Fold over the edge of the bag, then staple the handle to each side. Fill the bag with grass. The handle should be made out of thick card board paper. Boil the eggs one day before, then have the children color and decorate the eggs. Plan your Easter egg hunt before lunch and have your party after lunch. Use your eggs to make deviled eggs for lunch, children love them! Invite parents to your party, verbally. Most parents work, but there will be some that will show up, so be prepared.

Always celebrate the children's birthdays. Parents seem to appreciate it, when you show special attention to their child. Have the parent bring one box of cake mix and cool whip, you can supply the eggs and oil. Have cooking experience with the children in the morning and talk about who's birthday we are celebrating today.

Many children do not celebrate their birthday's at home. Many times it is because parents do not have the time to celebrate or just don't have the money. So celebrating their birthday at the center is a special event for everyone.

Buy border paper (trimming paper) with different designs, and make hats for them. Measure the children's heads with the border paper and them staple each end. After the party is over take the hats and put them away for the next party. I have pointed out the biggest events in which you should include your parents. These events help you and the parents to continue a close relationship. During these events there is time to socialize and just talk about the program in general. It is not a time to talk about Johnny's problems, please keep in mind.

14
PUTTING BINDER TOGETHER

Put together all the information about your program in a binder so that when you visit Referral Programs, schools, agencies and training centers you'll have it with you and ready to present. Take pictures of the children involved in different activities. People love to see happy children participating in activities.

The following forms should be included in your binder,

License
Training, experience, reference letters, certificates
Parents Handbook (Your rules & regulations)
Pictures of the children
Schedule of daily activities
Copy of Flyer
Copy of your membership to your local Family Day Care Association
Copy of membership to the Food Program

15
FAMILY DAY CARE ASSOCIATION AND REFERRAL PROGRAM AGENCIES

The family day care associations are a group of professional women that promote the developing recognition of quality home day care. They represent professionalism in the areas of child development and child care. They offer services that will strengthen your program. For example, workshops in child development, art activities, nutrition, health, CPR, bookkeeping and income tax preparation.

The association offers to its members subscription to the monthly newsletters, workshops, free referral services, discount on liability Insurance, updates on legislative issues and licensing mandates, and discounts on local businesses usually from 10–20% when you purchase something.

The monthly newsletter has excellent information that can be helpful to you when preparing your pre-school program, food program, or just informal information that will help you personally. The letter keeps you informed with local as well as state issues in day care.

I have found that the newsletter is an important tool to my business. It keeps me in contact with the outside world. It keeps me informed with what is going on in the community.

There is a joining fee, plus a yearly fee to join the association. This is used to pay for state membership, which we need to be part of, since they keep us informed of state legislation.

Many of us join the local family day care association just for the referral service they offer. We depend on the referrals, yet we don't participate in fund raisers, which keeps the association going. I believe we, as members, must be active in the association because it offers so much to us. Without the association we would find ourselves in great trouble, because we would lack contact with new legislation that is being developed for day care, referral service, local information, art activities being printed in the newsletter, and nutrition information that we can use and distribute to parents. We would also lack information on liability insurance and many more ideas helpful in order to maintain our business in a professional manner. Being a member to these excellent day care associations is a plus to your business, believe me! Be an active member, and you will find yourself happier and feel that you are a professional in day care.

The day care referral programs are agencies that refer day care to you. Most of these agencies are funded by the state. You automatically are put on their referral list when your license is approved through social services.

There is no cost to you for being part of the agency, because like I said, they are funded by the state.

The referral agencies also offer other services besides day care referral. They offer workshops on a variety of areas, child care, nutrition, drug awareness, child abuse prevention, alcoholism, health, etc. They do referral for people that need help in a particular area. They also offer a Toy Lending Library program for home providers.

The Toy Lending Library is utilized mostly by home providers. I think it is a great program for us, since the services are free, plus they have excellent toys to check out. Remember earlier in the book I explained that the Toy Lending Library was a great service to us because it gives the opportunity to renew the toys every week. The Toy Lending Library is for you!

The Family Day care association and referral programs are excellent programs that you should take advantage of. They are there for you!

CONCLUSION

A home provider is a person that offers day care services in their home. It is a special person that is loving, caring, intelligent, and willing to continue to learn about children in order to develop their program professionally.

Being a home provider is very rewarding because you play the role of a mother to these children. Children are being trusted over to you by parents that are desperate in finding quality day care for their precious little ones. You not only play the role of a mother but also a teacher. You teach the children how to cope with life in general.

You must be able to be considerate toward the needs of the child by being a loving and touching person. Give a child a hug or maybe a kiss on the cheek, just to let the child know it is okay and that he/she can count on you.

A combination of training, consideration and love is the best recipe for being a successful home provider.

I hope that by writing this book it will help thousands of home providers that find themselves desperate for answers to their questions. Now that you have read my book you feel better about yourself and about the profession you chose. You will see yourself as a professional, with the incentive to continue.

I believe that this book can help anyone to be successful in day care profession. Because of its simplicity, anyone can read and follow it.

Remember to keep your book handy. Place your book near an area where you can see it, and be able to reach it quickly if you need it!

This book is like a recipe book, a dictionary and an encyclopedia. It is your bible to your business. Remember to make copies of all the forms I have developed.

I hope that you find this book as useful as I have. I hope you will enjoy reading it as much as I enjoyed writing it. Good luck in your day care profession, and I know now since you read my book, you are excited and willing to try.

RESOURCES LISTS

MY FAVORITE STORY BOOKS FOR CHILDREN

Be My Valentine, Charlie Brown, Charles M. Schulz (Random House)
Love Is a Special Way of Feeling, Joan Walsh Anglund (Harcourt Brace Jovanovich)
Be My Valentine, Miriam Cohen
The Browing Tree
The Three Billy Goats Gruff, Peter Christian Asbjornsen
Where the Wild Things Are, Maurice Sendak
The House That Jack Built, Paul Galdone
The Little Red Hen, Galdone
Brown Bear, Brown Bear What Do You See?, Bill Martin Jr. (Henry Holt Co.)
Silly Goose, Omerod
I Can't Said the Ant, Polly Cameron (Scholastic)
I Hate to Take a Bath, Judi Barrett (Modern Promotions Publications)
Anabelle Swift, Kindergartner, Schwartz
Bathtime, Jean Bethell (Holt)
The Strawberry Book of Colors, Richard Heffer
Adventures of Three Colors, Annette Tison and Talus Taylor
In the Rain, Anne Rockwell
It Looked Like Split Milk, Charles Shaw
Hello Clouds!, Dalia Renberg
All Fall Down, Helen Oxenbury
Growing, Fiona Pragoff
Biggest Snowstorm Ever, Diane Paterson

Josie and the Snow, Helen Buckley
The Snowman, Jan Orskine
When Will It Snow?, Syd Hoff
The Ballooning Adventure of Paddy Pork, John Goodall
Who Likes it Hot?, Mary Garlick
Why You Feel Hot, Why You Feel Cold: Your Body's Temperature, James Barry
Pete's Pup, Kathy's Kitty, Syd Holt
What Do You Do With a Kangaroo?, Mercer Mayer
The Bear's Toothache, David McPhail
Old McDonald Had a Farm, Moritz Kennel
The Farmer in the Dell, Mary Maki Rae (Scholastic)
Oh What a Mess!, Wilhelm
Corduroy, Don Freeman (Viking and Penguin)
Elbert's Bad Word, Audrey Wood
Boy with a Problem, Joan Fassler (Human Science Press)
The Three Bears Rhyme Book, Yolen
Oh Lewis, Eve Rice (Penguin 1979)
Tortillas Para Mama, Margo Griego
Don't Touch, Suzy Kline (Albert Whitman)
Green Eggs and Ham, Dr. Seuss (Random House)
Round and Round the Garden, Moira Kemp
Popcorn, Frank Asch (Parent Magazine Press)
Put Me in the Zoo, Robert Lopshire
The Rainbow, Mike Thaler
Bears on Wheels, Stan and Jan Berenstain
Is It Red? Is It Yellow? Is It Blue?, Tana Hoban
One Fish, Two Fish, Red Fish, Blue Fish, Dr. Seuss
Colors, Jean Pientowski
My First Book of Things, John E. Johnson
Alexander and the Terrible, Horrible, No Good, Very Bad Day
Naughty Nancy, John Gooddall (Atheneum)
Stone Soup, Marcia Brown (Macmillan)
Pancakes for Breakfast, Tomie DePaola (Harcourt Brace Jovonavich)
Bread and Cheese, David Lloyd
IF This My Dinner, Irma Simonton Black
Food, Sarah Lyn
Know Your Fruits, Know Your Vegetables, Jules Books
Josie and the Snow, Helen Buckley (Lothrop Lee and Shepard)

In the Rain, Anne Rockwell
Oh Dear Dear Zoo, Rod Campbell (Four Winds Press 1983)
On Our Way to the Zoo, Harriet Ziefert and Simmons Taback (Harper and Row, 1985)
Oh That Cat, Norman Simon (Albert Whitman)
Pet Store, Peter Spier
Is It Larger, Is It Smaller?, Tana Hoban
My Five Senses, Aliki
Big or Little, Kathy Stinson and Robin Baird Lewis
Big or Little, Ruth Krauss
Good Night Moon, Brown
The Little Engine That Could, Piper
The Carrot Seed, Ruth Krauss
Thump-Thump Rat-a-Tat-Tat, Gene Baer
Baby Bear's Bedtime Book, Jane Yolen
Little Blue and Little Yellow, Leo Lionni
I Read Signs, Tana Hoban
Spot on the Farm, Eric Hill
Kitten from One to Ten, Mirra Ginsberg
Are You My Mommy?, Philip D. Eastman
Ask Mr. Bear, Marjorie Flack
Book of Nursery and Mother Goose Rhymes, Marguerite DeAngeli
Things That Go, Ann Rockwell
Animals on the Farm, Feodor Rojankovsky
Airport, Byron Barton
Baby Says, John Steptoe
Chicken Little, Steven Kellogg
Curious George, Hans Augusto Rey
Rain Makes Applesauce, Julian Scheer
The Cat in the Hat, Dr. Seuss
I Am Going On a Bear Hunt, Sandra Stroner Sivulich
Caps for Sale, Esphyr Slobodkina
Little Toot, Hardie Gramatky
My Mother Travels a Lot, Bauer
Make Way for Ducklings, McCloskey
Mother Goose: A Treasury of Best-Loved Rhymes, Illustrated by Tim and Greg Hildebrandt, Edited by Watty Piper

BOOKS THAT CAN HELP YOU WITH YOUR PRE-SCHOOL PROGRAM

Things to Do with Toddlers and Twos, Karen Miller
Activities Learning for Twos, Debby Cvyer, Thelma Harms and Beth Bourland
Science Fun, Imogene Forte (Incentive Publications)
Teaching Terrific Twos, Terry Lynne Braham and Linda Camp (Humanic Learning)
Look at Me, Activities for Babies and Toddlers, Carolyn Buhai Haas
Music for Ones and Twos, Tom Glazer
Come and Get It, Kathleen Baxter
Cooking With Kids, Cardine Ackerman
Baby Games, Elaine Martin
1-2-3-Art, Jean Warren
Splish, Splash, Yvonne Hooker
Let's Look for Surprises All Around, Harold Roth
Shapes, Shapes, Shapes, Tana Hoban
Whose Hat?, Margaret Miller
Fire Engine Shapes, Bruce Mcmillan
The Block Book, Elizabeth Hirsch
Block Building, Esther Starkes
Block City, Robert Louis Stevenson
Read-Aloud Rhymes for Young, Jack Prelutsky
Learning Through Cooking, Nancy Ferreira
Cooking with Kids, Caroline Ackerman
Feeling Strong, Feeling Free: Movement Exploration for Young Children, Molly Sullivan
Come and Get It: A Natural Foods Cookbook for Children, Kathleen Baxter

BOOKS TO SHARE WITH PARENTS

Liberated Parents-Liberated Children, Avon
How to Talk So Kids Will Listen and Listen So Kids Will Talk, Avon
Self-Esteem, A Family Affair, Jean I. Clark
Siblings Without Rivalry, Adele Faber and Elaine Mazlish
Without Spanking or Spoiling, A Practical Approach to Toddler and Pre-school Guidance, Elizabeth Crary
Your Child's Self-Esteem, Dorothy C. Briggs
Toddlers and Parents: Declaration of Independence, T. Berry Brazelton
Toddler Years, Edited by Dodie Schultz and Parents Magazine Editors.
Your Toddler, Richard Run, John Fisher and Susan Doering
Your Two-Year-Old, Terrible or Tender, Louise Bates Ames and Frances Ilg
The Whole Child, Joanne Hendrick

MY FAVORITE VIDEOS

All Barney's Tape Series
All Disney Sing-A-Longs
Baby Songs, Hi Top Video
All Disney Classics
All Sesame Street Videos
Finger Plays for Little Ones, Mary Clever
Videos may be used as fillers:
  Examples:
    When you are busy making lunch and you want the children to sit quiet.
    On Rainy Days.
      Arrival time—when children are arriving in the morning and you are busy greeting the parents and children.
      At the end of the day. Parents are picking up the children and you are busy talking with the parents.

POISONOUS HOUSEHOLD ITEMS USED DAILY

Bleaches
Oven cleaners
Glue
Nail polish
Polish remover
Hair spray
Perfumes
Room spray
Mothballs
Fertilizer
Bubble bath
Baby powder

Gasoline
Weed killers
Tylenol
Aspirin
Baby Aspirin
Vitamins
Comet and Ajax
Clothes soap
Dish soap
Furniture polish
Floor polish

INJURY PREVENTION

By a Choke Tester so that you are able to test small objects.
Throw away broken toys and equipment.
Keep pins and nails, toothpicks, paper clips, tacks, staples on a high area.
Pick up hazardous objects.
Don't give styroform cups to babies.
Don't wear long dangly jewelry.
Don't ever prop an infant bottle when feeding.
Always check pacifiers to see if they are loose.
Don't let children run with things in their mouths.
Don't let children put pencils in their mouths.
Don't feed babies hard vegetables and candies.
Train children to walk with pointed side of scissors in the palm of the hand.

COMMON POISONOUS PLANTS

Hyacinth
Tobacco
Baneberry
Ivy
Jasmine
Mistletoe
Elephant ear
Shamrock
Iris
Buttercups

Mushrooms
Tomato leaves
Potato leaves
Poinsettia
Holly
Azalea
Philodendron
Daffodils
Lily of the valley
Black locust

COMMON SAFE PLANTS

Pussy willow
Moss
Rose
Lilac
Honeysuckle
Boston fern
Pine cone seeds
Wandering Jew

Rubber plant
Begonia
Jade plant
Spider plant
Swedish ivy
Artichoke
Rubber plant
Yucca

FOODS THAT CAUSE CHILDREN TO CHOKE AND SUFFOCATE

Hard candy
Lollipops
Gum
Popcorn
Raw carrots
Raw celery
Raw apples
Peanuts

Chips
Hot dogs
Peanut butter
Raisins
Grapes with skin
Nuts
Cherries
Yogurt with nuts

TOYS THAT CAN CAUSE CHILDREN TO CHOKE AND SUFFOCATE

- Balloons
- Beads
- Play jewelry
- Jacks
- Marbles
- Tokens
- Rubber bands
- Tiny toys
  - (Polly Pocket)
  - (Barbie toys)
- Baby barrettes
- Tiny balls
- Broken crayons

PREVENTING THE SPREAD OF CHILDHOOD ILLNESSES

Wash toys regularly. Have children wash toys; they love it!
Diaper changer must be close to a sink.
Have a tight diaper dispenser and empty regularly throughout the day.
Wash blankets at least once a week.
Give each child his own blanket and mat.
Do not pile blankets and jackets. Blankets must be folded and placed in cubbies. Jackets must be hung on coat hangers.
Wash bathroom regularly with bleach.
Aways wash hands after diaper change, or cleaning a child after a bowel movement.
Separate children who are ill from children who are not.
Clean mat and wash blanket after ill child leaves.
Spray disinfectant in the areas where children are daily.
Have children wash hands before eating.
Mop the kitchen area regularly.
Wash dishes in bleach.

GLOSSARY

Affidavit Regarding Liability Insurance
A form that tells parents that the provider does not carry liability insurance.

Art Activities,
Activities that include glue, paints, crayons, paper, scissors, etc.

Bulletin Board
An area on the wall where important information for the parents is posted.

Cognitive Development
The ability to knowing and understanding.

Criminal Release Form
Release giving permission to obtain a criminal record for employment purposes.

Cubbies
An area where each child can put their belongings in.

Daily Schedule
A schedule of daily routines that the center follows throughout the day.

Discipline Rules
Rules that you expect children to follow when they are under your care. Also a reminder to you on how to discipline children the correct way.

Dramatic Center
An area where children are given the opportunity to develop social skills. It is an area that has dress up clothes, a kitchen set, dolls, telephone, typewriter, etc.

Emotional Development
Emotions that contribute to the child's inner sense of self-direction.

Facility Roster
A form where names of children are accumulated that attend day care.

Finger-Play
Songs that permit the use of fingers when singing.

Fingerprint Cards
Fingerprints that are obtained at Sheriff's Office for purpose of employment or other reasons.

Fire Exit Plan
A plan of the house showing exits out in case of a fire. This plan tells you how to exit and where to go with the children.

Food Bank
A program where home providers are allowed to shop for food by the pounds. This is available to foster parents, group homes, and home providers that offer day care to low income children.

Food Enrollment Form
This form states that the child is participating in a food program.

Food Program
A variety of food programs that are being funded by the Federal Government to assist day care with food cost.

Home Provider
Is a person that offers day care, with a pre-school program in their own home.

Identification Emergency Form
A form where people are being listed by the parents as responsible persons in case of emergencies and parents cannot be reached.

In-House Training
Training within the program that is offered to employees to improve skills.

Language Development
The beginning of connecting sounds. Meaningful sounds as produced by the action of the vocal organs.

Medical Treatment Form
It gives the right to the caretaker to take the child to hospital for emergency treatment that is necessary to preserve the life of the child.

Need Assessment Forms
Forms that show the growing progress of the child.

Parents' Handbook
A booklet developed for parents that states rules and regulations of the program.

Parents' Rights
The parents obtain the right to enter and inspect the day care where their children are being cared for.

Personal Rights
The form states that the parents have the right to report any possible child abuse they feel is going on at the facility that their child is being cared for.

Physical Development
The growth of the body through proper care.

Play Dough
Dough that children use to make objects with. This is excellent in developing small muscles.

Pre-School
Constituting the period in the child's life from infancy to the age of five or six that ordinarily precedes attendance at elementary school.

Pre-School Curriculum
Pre-school activities that are put together so teachers can use when teaching pre-schoolers. Activities are developed according to age level.

Protection Gates
Gates that are child proof and are used to illuminate a child from entering a certain area.

Recipe Cards
Large cards that show recipes that children can follow when doing cooking experience.

Science Center
It is an area where science activities are being experienced.

Sign-In/Sign-Out Sheet
A form where parents sign their name, time and date they bring and pick-up their child for day care.

Social Development
The ability to interact with others.

Social Services
These are services offered to people in the area of drug health, child abuse, nutrition, counseling, etc.

T.B. Test
Skin test to determine if the person has tuberculosis.

Water Activities
Activities that are done in water.

Workmen's Compensation
Liability Insurance for Employees.